Contents

- Poetry:

- Photography

-

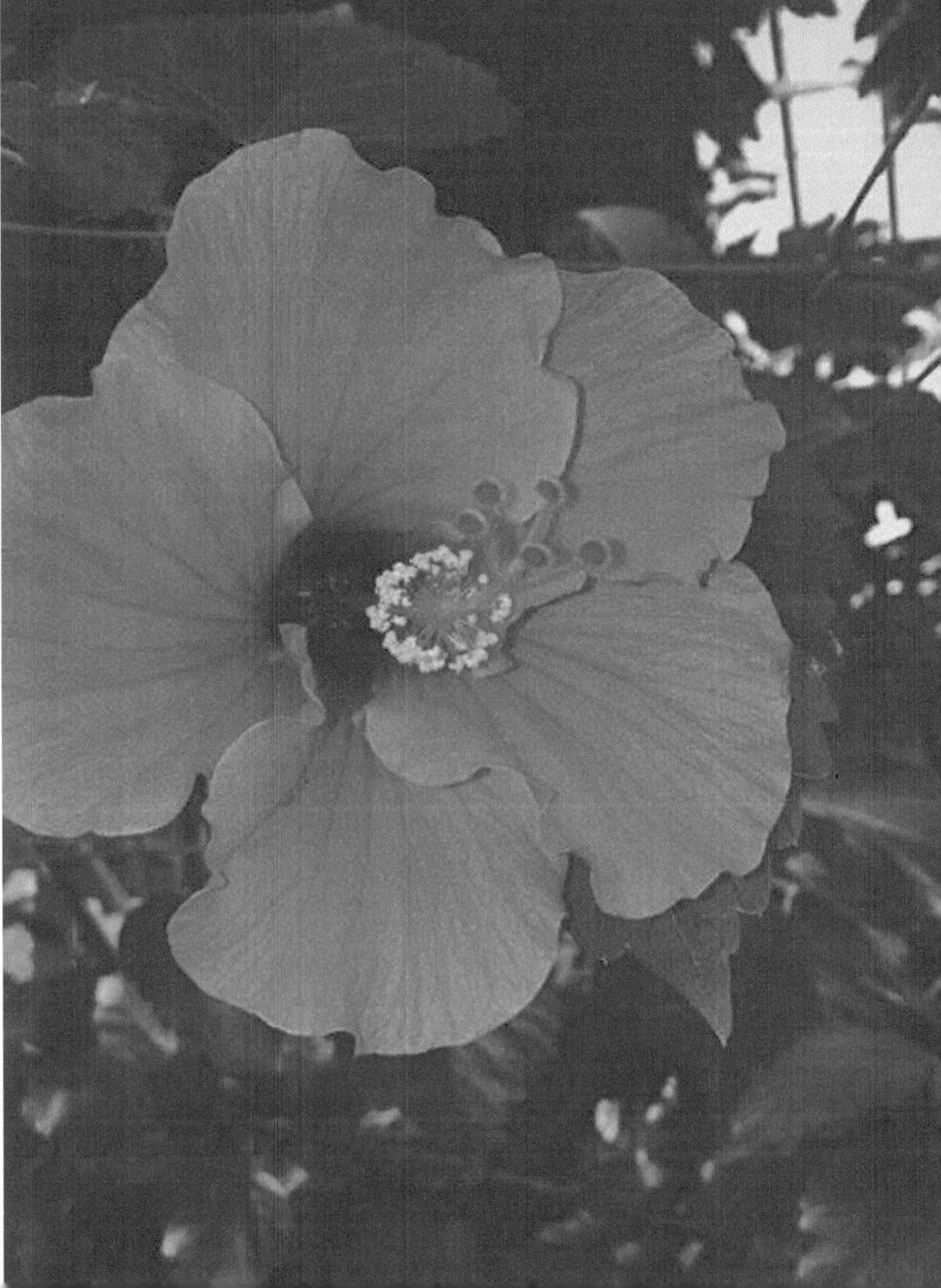

st. cloud

laying on a blanket of damp earth
beneath thick fog
guarded by marble angels and the stoic,
immobile trees
they use each other for warmth
though it's really not that cold

absentmindedly, he grabs a fistful of needles
buried in the emerald ground and tosses them
in her hair
despite her reaction, she isn't angry at all
honestly, she is under his spell

they move closer together and stare at the sky,
and all she can think is how she could
catch the moon, that's how high she feels

he looks over and can see the twinkling lights
in her chocolate eyes and is reminded of why
he loves her

he kissed her softly, lips tasting of peppermint
bliss, burned as if by electrical charge

though it seems to have lasted only a few
seconds, they open their eyes to the first
light of the new day and think,
what a strange and magical place for ghosts to
fall in love.

honey

i couldn't feel my heart for a minute there.
and i wasn't scared because i could feel
everything.
i felt my heart and the heat that radiated
to
every piece of my mind.
there is light everywhere
and through the pain,
i feel a smile work it's way up
til it reaches my face.
a small piece of happiness in the warmth
of a soft embrace
and i start to think
that possibly i can be whole again.

a love poem in spanish

dicen que español es el lenguaje del amor
                    pero
pienso que es la manera tus ojos miran
                    en mios
y tus labios darme besos, siempre.

sus ojos son como el mar,
azul, y verde, y oro
son los dos calma y aspero
hermosos per impactante

si yo fuera un artista,
tu cuerpo seria mi lienzo
en que pintar, con mis labios
con dedos frios y aliento calido

tu risa y tu sonrisa
pusieron un fuego en mi corazon
me dejas sin aliento
con la forma en que hablas
y la forma en que nos movemos
como uno.

mirame
estoy vivo con amor
tan seguro como la luna ama el sol

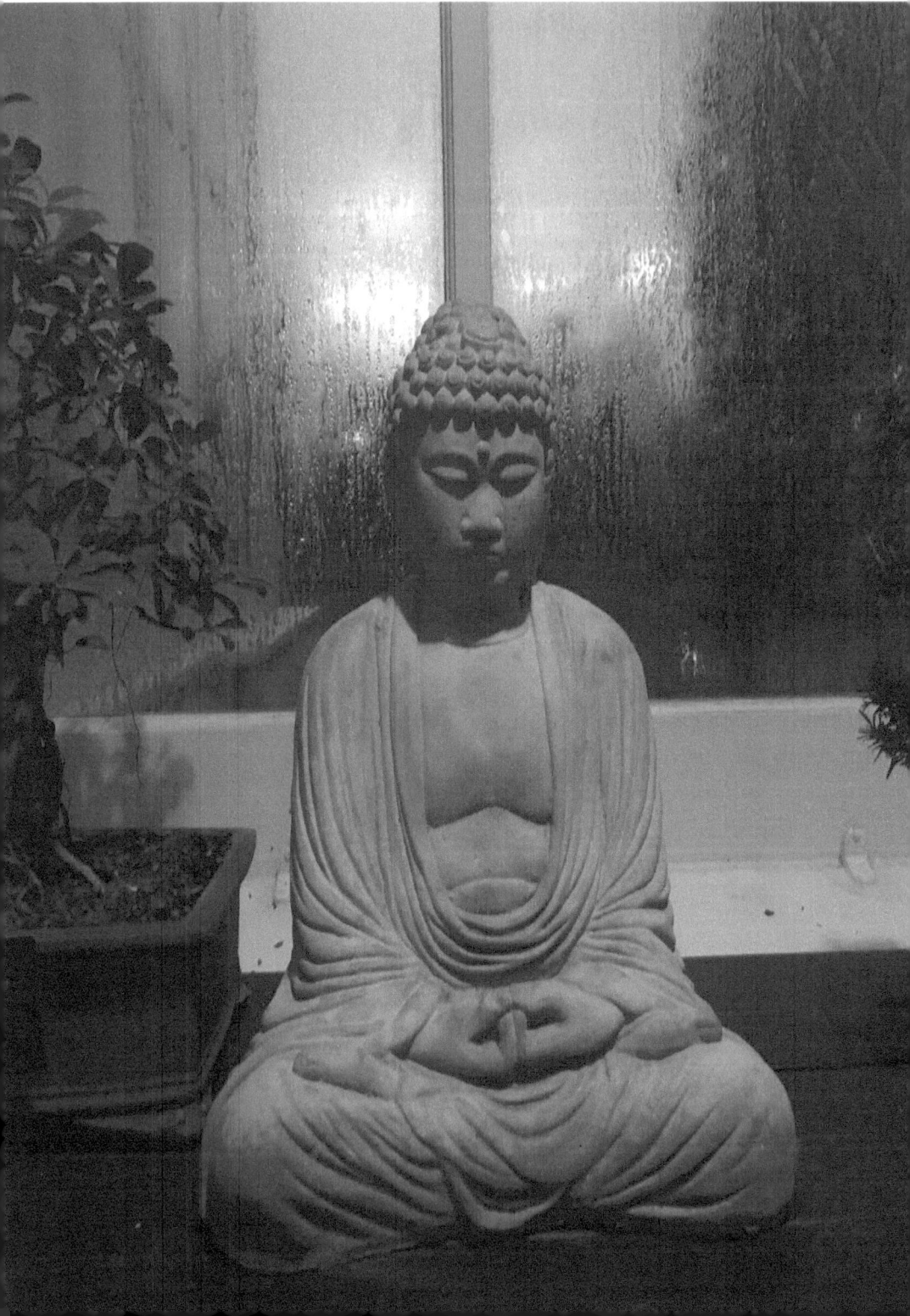

woman power

the day i let a
    man
dictate my entire life
is the day i give
  someone
permission to put a
    bullet
in my empty head

goodbye/hello

i have always hated goodbyes.
the finality
the emptiness of words unspoken
a flash of memories leaves a
blank space in
my mind
once so full, no longer
is there a way to make goodbye
feel like hello?
because i have always loved hellos.
the beauty
the freshness of a new start
a glimpse of things to come
filling the blank space
in my mind
for sometimes you have to say
goodbye
if you want to find a new
hello.

me too.

naivety by its very definition is the
lack
of wisdom, experience, or judgement
youth as a time in one's life
gives birth to the wide-eyed, jaw dropping
beauty that comes with the unknown

so i was young.
and naive.
so then i must have deserved what followed.

he was an excellent musician.
in fact, i could have listened to him play for hours.
and it was the first time i felt a love like that.

i agreed to it.
i couldn't feel anything, numb to most of the pain,
as you whispered in my ear, "you're a trooper"
whatever you gave me...i need more. so i can forget.

he worked two jobs to pay the bills.
he had kind eyes and played soccer like me.
and who could ignore the appeal of a guy with an
accent?

i needed it.
i was bored and lonely and wanted somewhere to go.
and i felt, of my dignity being torn apart
and i need more tissues for all the tears and the blood.

he was an amazing athlete.
he understood my humor but i never meant to
lead you on.

i wanted it.
in sweatpants and a t-shirt, hair a mess
as i bit into my hand to keep me silent, tears streaming
down my face.

i have grown older, wiser, and the more i understand
about the world, the less i understand about
this.

why would you take a broken girl and
break her more?
how could you hear her cry and know
you were the reason?
what part of you felt so entitled to
this piece of me that you just
took it?

you are from women
who are strong yet, gentle
wise, yet curious
fierce, yet beautiful

and you are mistaken
no.
naive,
to think this is not a woman's world
because you are from women
and guess what?

me too.

a dream in italian

queste parole cadono dalla mia lingua
come la rugiada su una foglia
dolcezza senza sforzo
in un mondo dove l'amarezza **è**
l'unico sapore
e come se fossi di nuovo un bambino
la bellezza **è** travolgente
il sole in tutta la sua gloria
balla nel cielo
Sono senza peso in questo paradiso
Vedo la luce più luminosa
      e
all'improvviso
i miei occhi aperti
sono a letto, da solo.
fuori, sta piovendo.
il cielo e grigio.
il sogno e finito.

tempo per illavoro.

obscurity

you are in love with a dying girl
she is trying to kill herself
without even trying
but she won't let you know that
she'll still love you
she'd do anything for you
she'll even kiss you
though that might take her last breath
til death do us part

silver screen

there is something so inherently
regal
about watching the big screen
words boom and echo with the power
of a wild thunderstorm
it's almost impossible to tear
my eyes away
the pure seduction
of seeing a whole new world come to
life
in two or three hours
a moving story can be told
sitting in a chair yet going on
countless adventures
our curiosity satisfied as,
momentarily,
we are able to escape our own
reality

spirit of hawaii

'O wau ke kaikamahine o ka moana
Ua ulu ka lā'au pāma i loko o ku'u pu'uwai
Ke holo nei ke kai ma ku'u mau'i'o
e honi ka makani i ko'u papalina
o ka mokupuni, he wahi l huna'ia
he'ina wau e like me ka lua pele
ua hau'oli wau e like me ka niu
ua nani wau e like me ka pua hibiscus

my big fat italian family

i am bold like my sister
strong like my mother
but gentle like mi nonna
i am smart like my cousins
and fierce like all of them

i am determined like my uncles
with charisma like my cousins
self–made like mi nonno
and resilient like all of them

i am from love and strength
from a shoulder to cry on and food on the table
i am from family and family is from me.

persephone

a daughter, born of flowers and warmth
kept pure and innocent for so long
with ethereal beauty, yet not a prize
to be won
or a quest to be conquered
stolen from this world
by a god of darkness and flames,
to be kept hidden from the light
for months
at first hurt, and lonely, soon
to find a small comfort in
a realm of sadness and fire
proof that beauty can blossom,
even where sun does not shine.
cursed to remain here but
blessed to be adored, if only
for a short while
and soon she realizes
it wasn't the worst mistake
to eat the ever so tempting
seeds of a single ruby red
pomegranate.

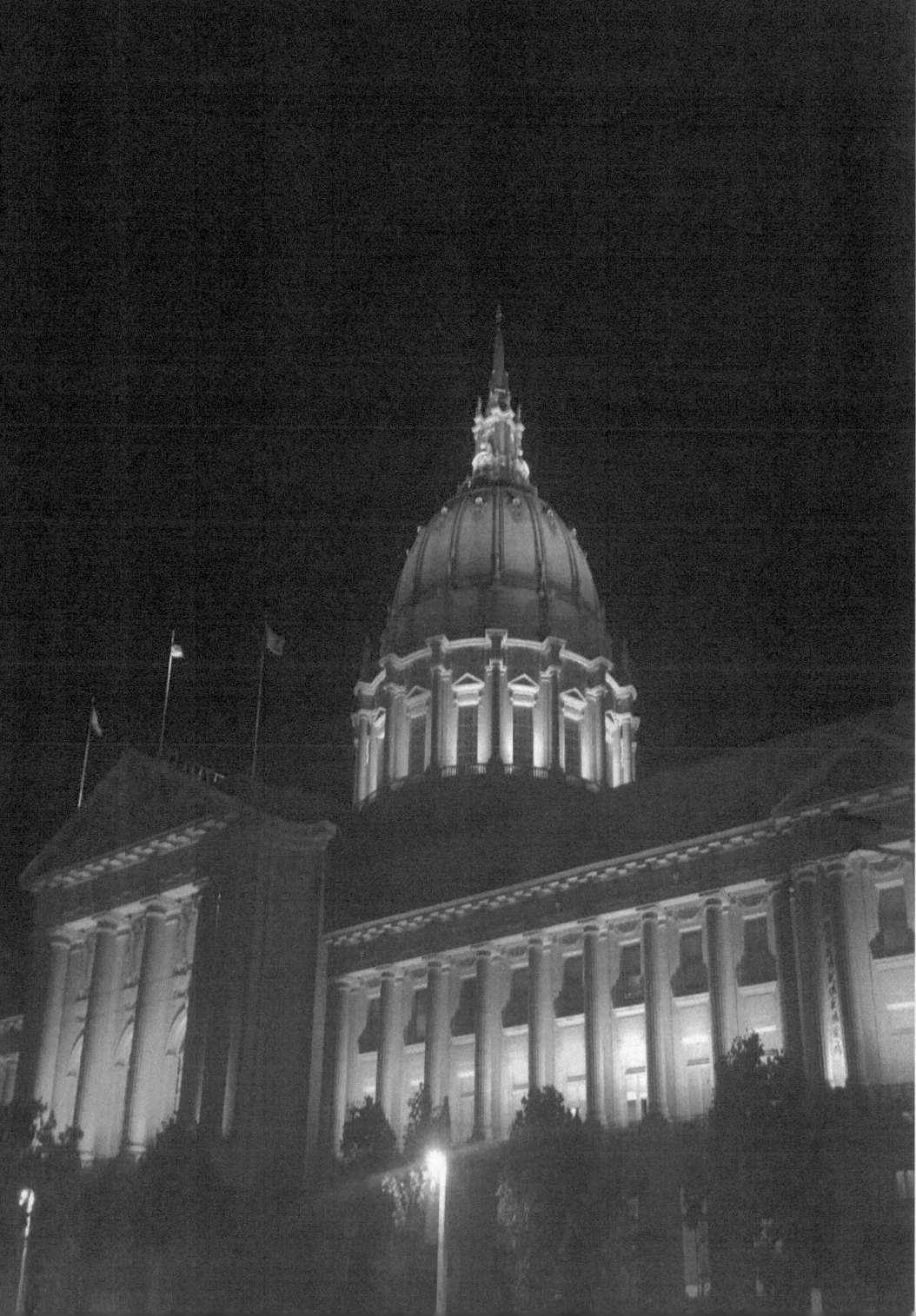

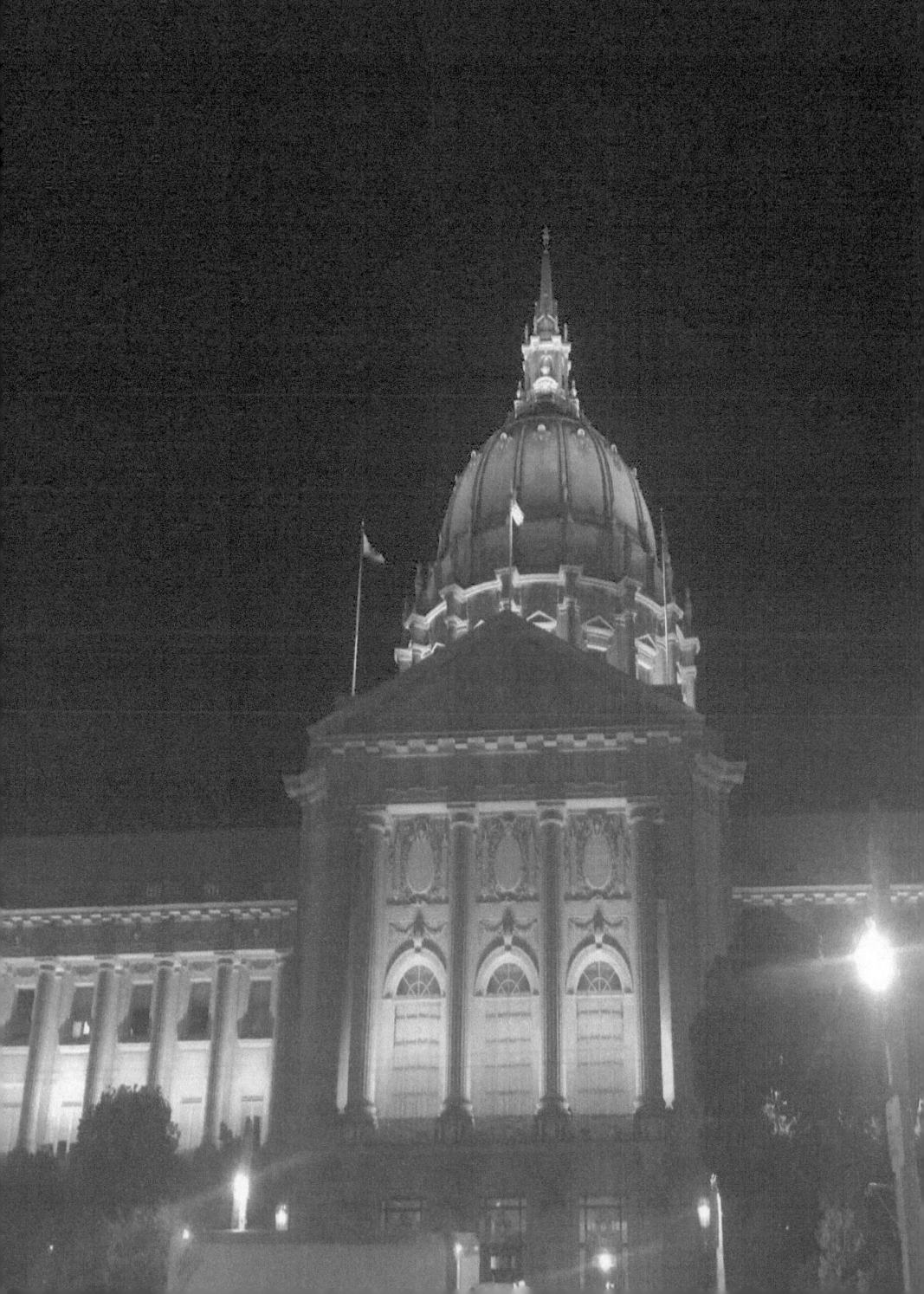

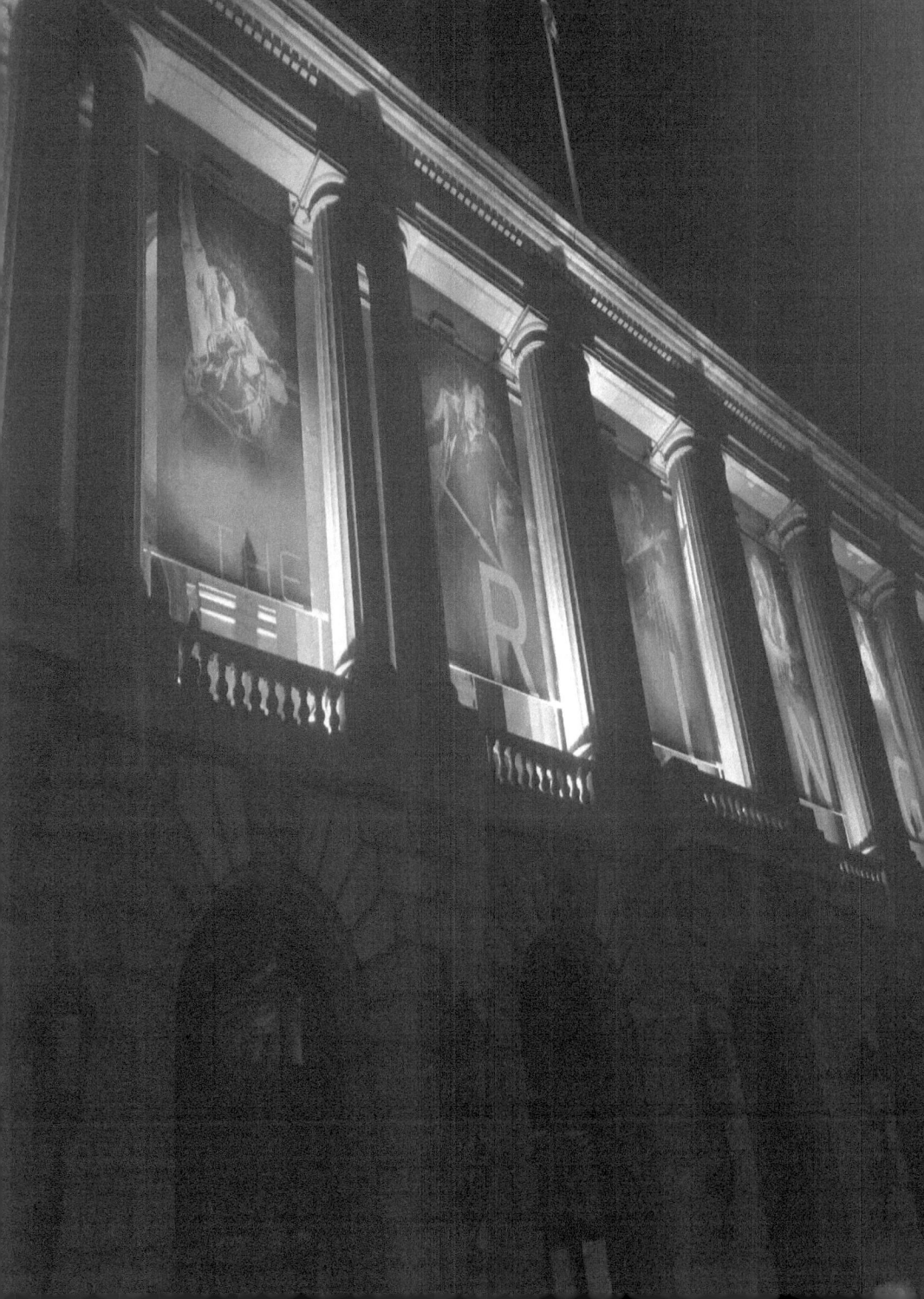

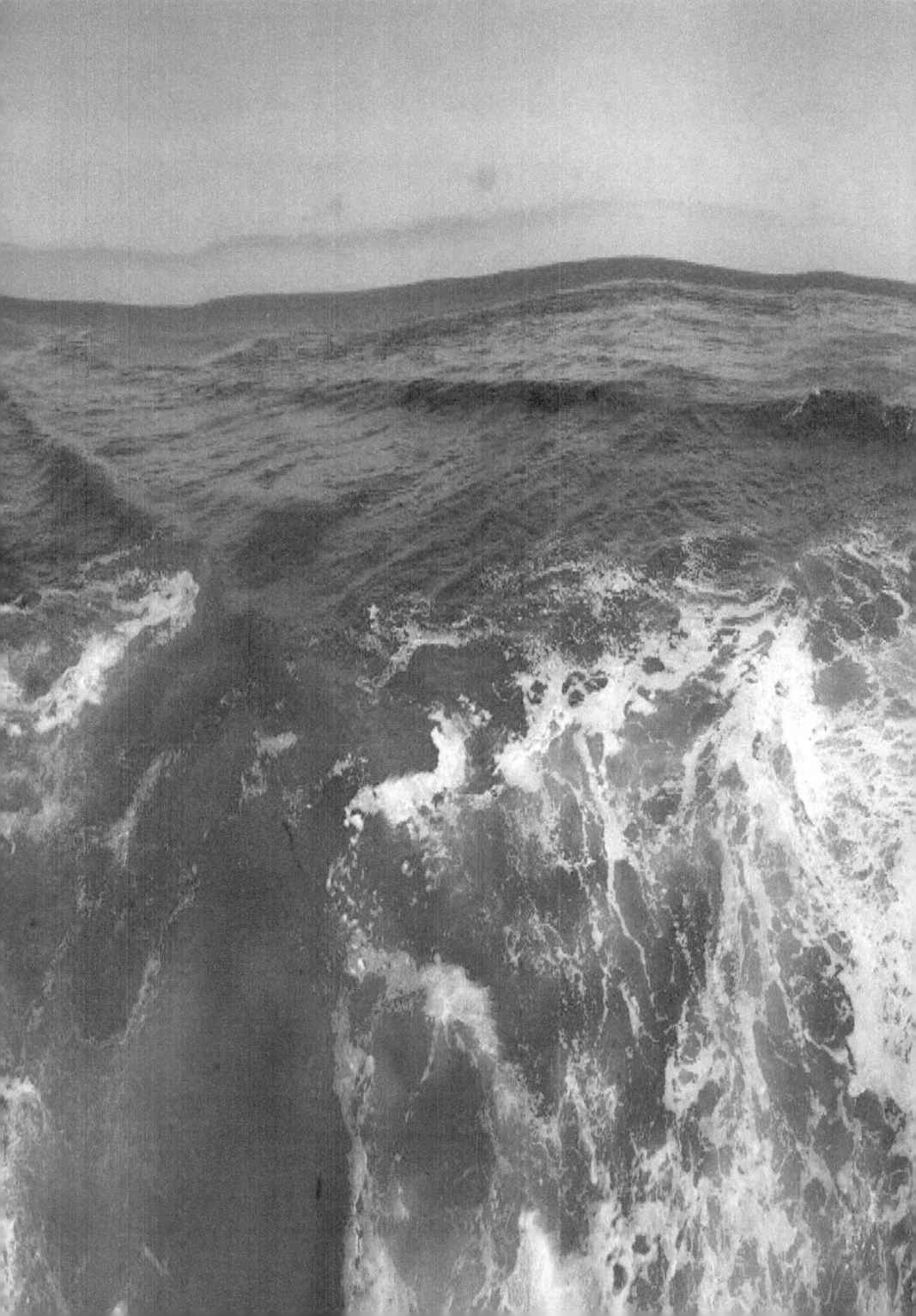

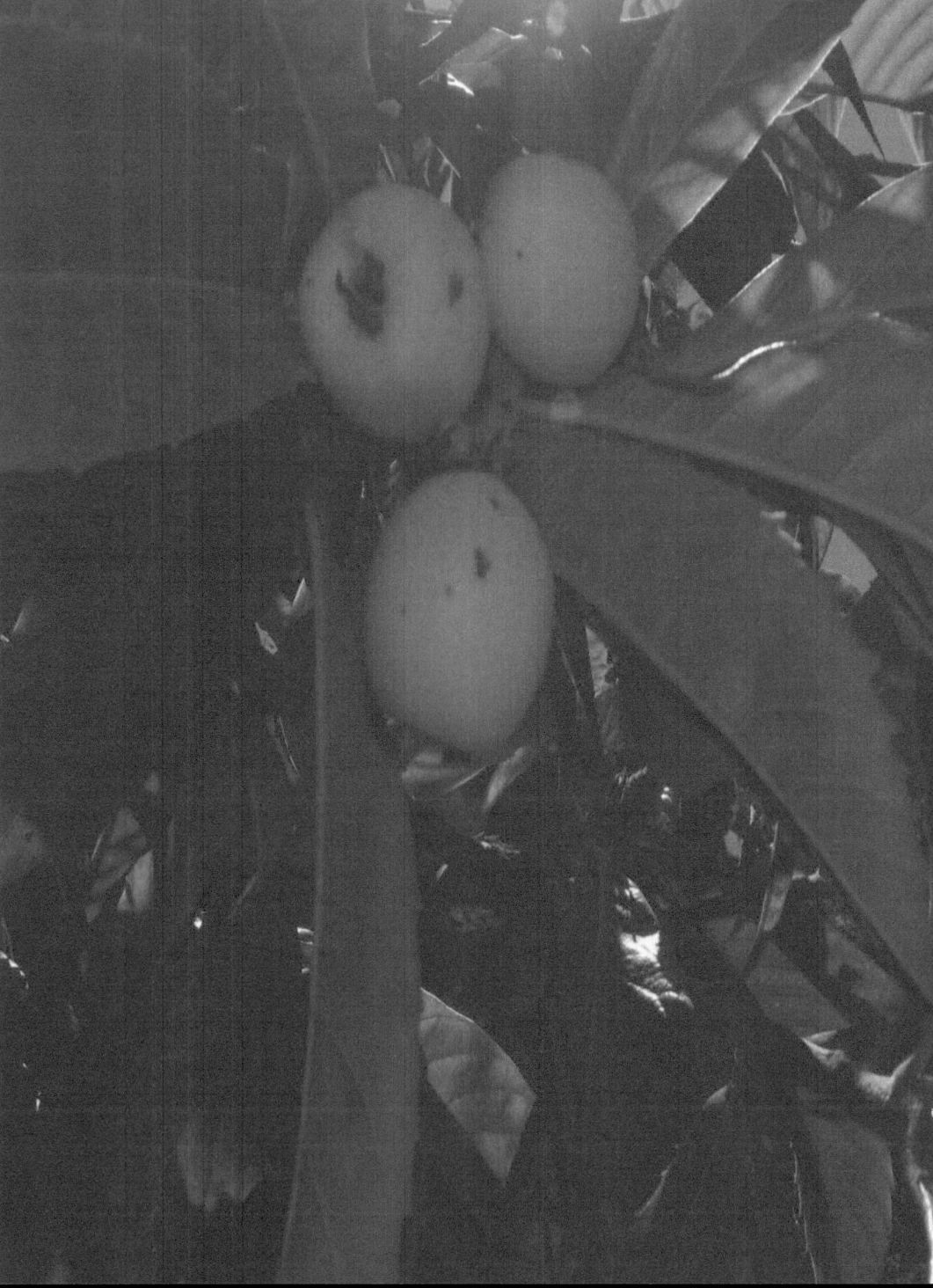

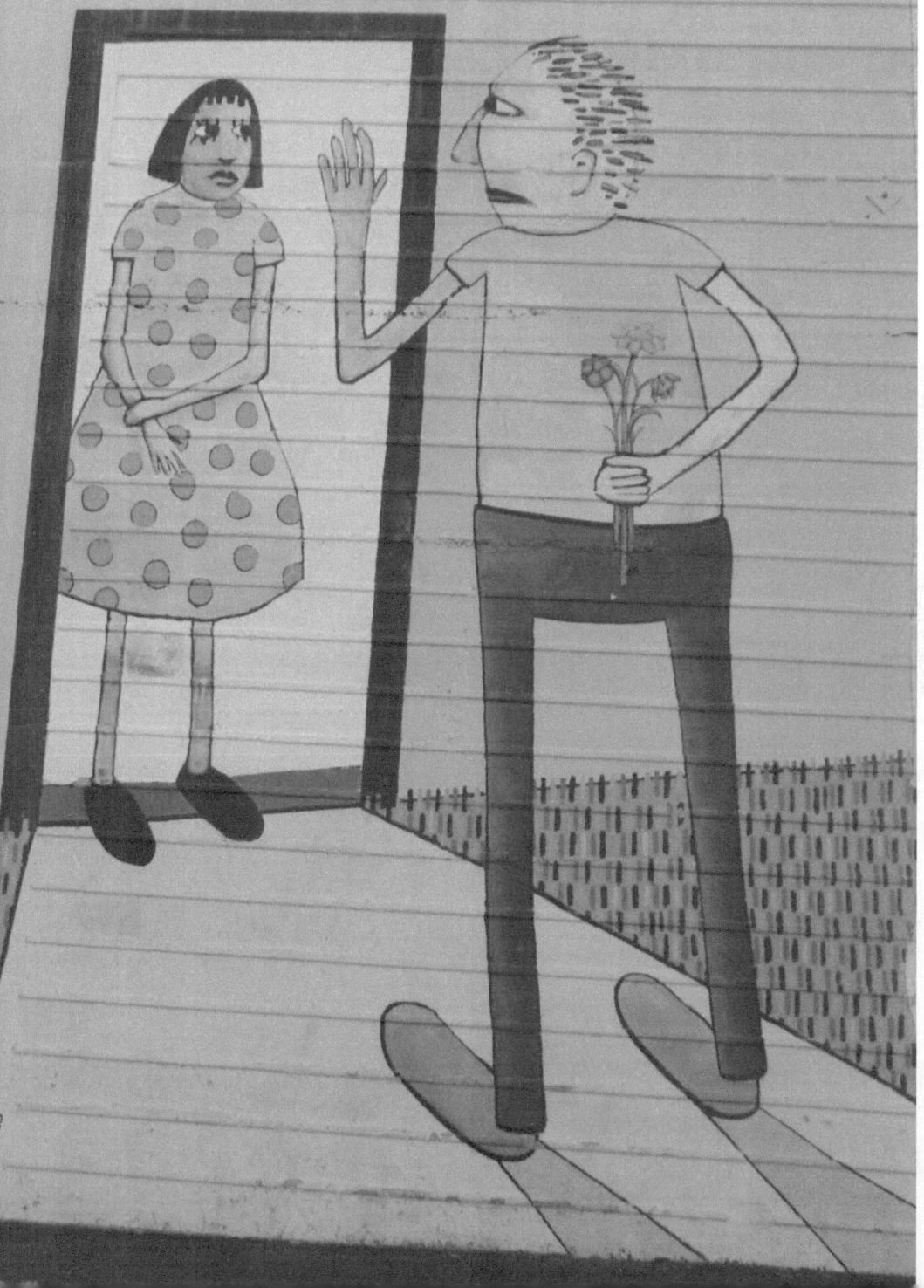

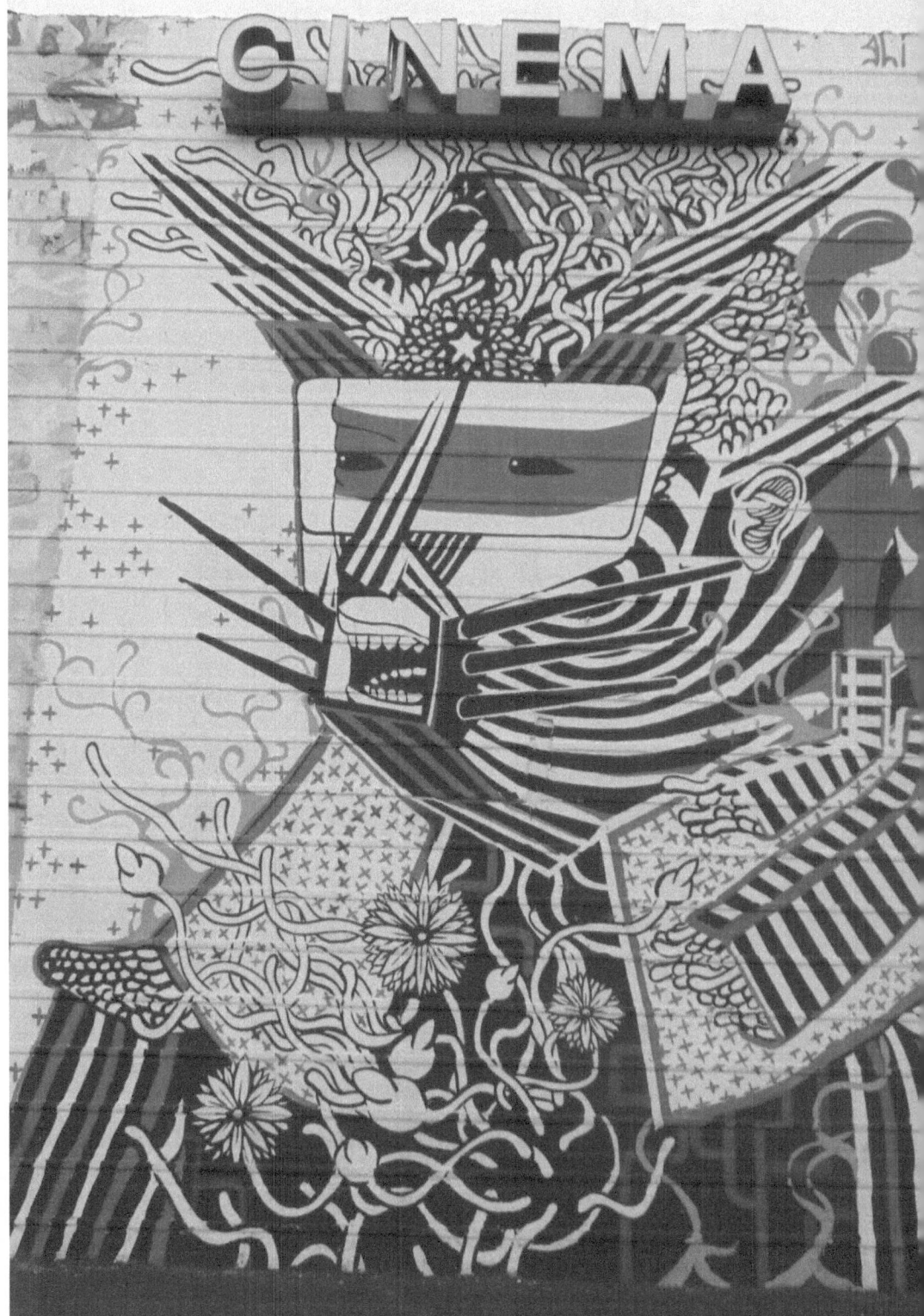

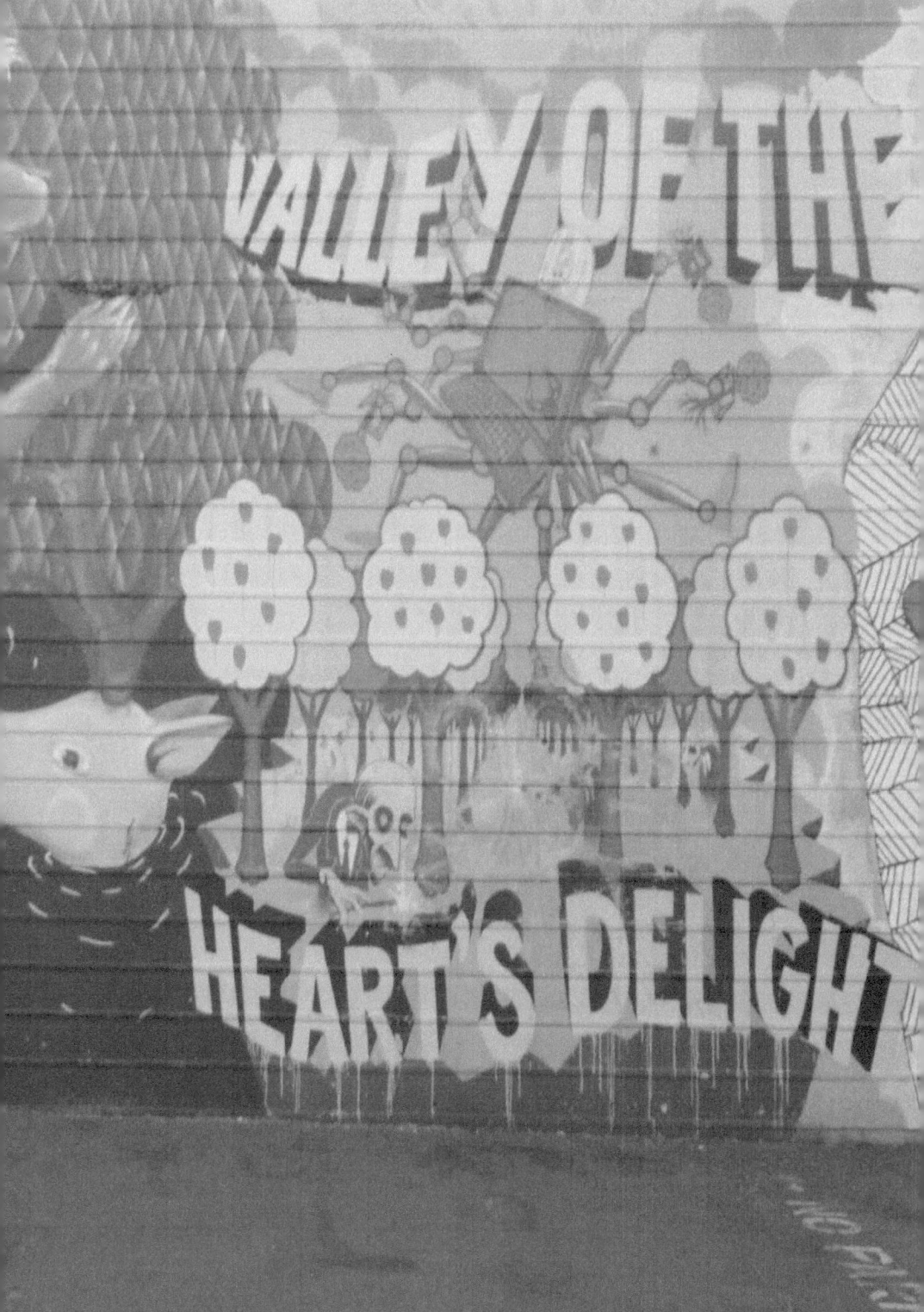

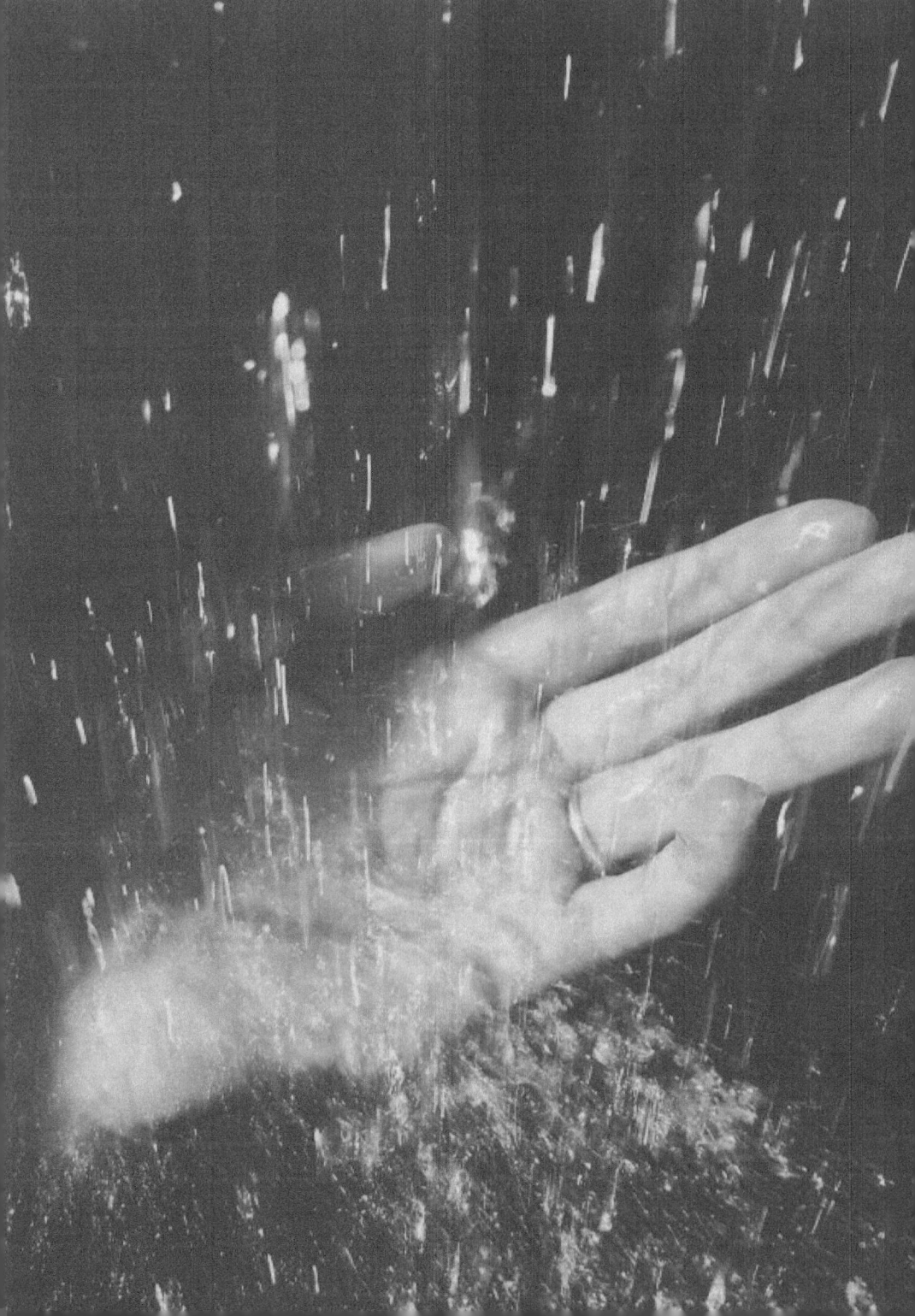

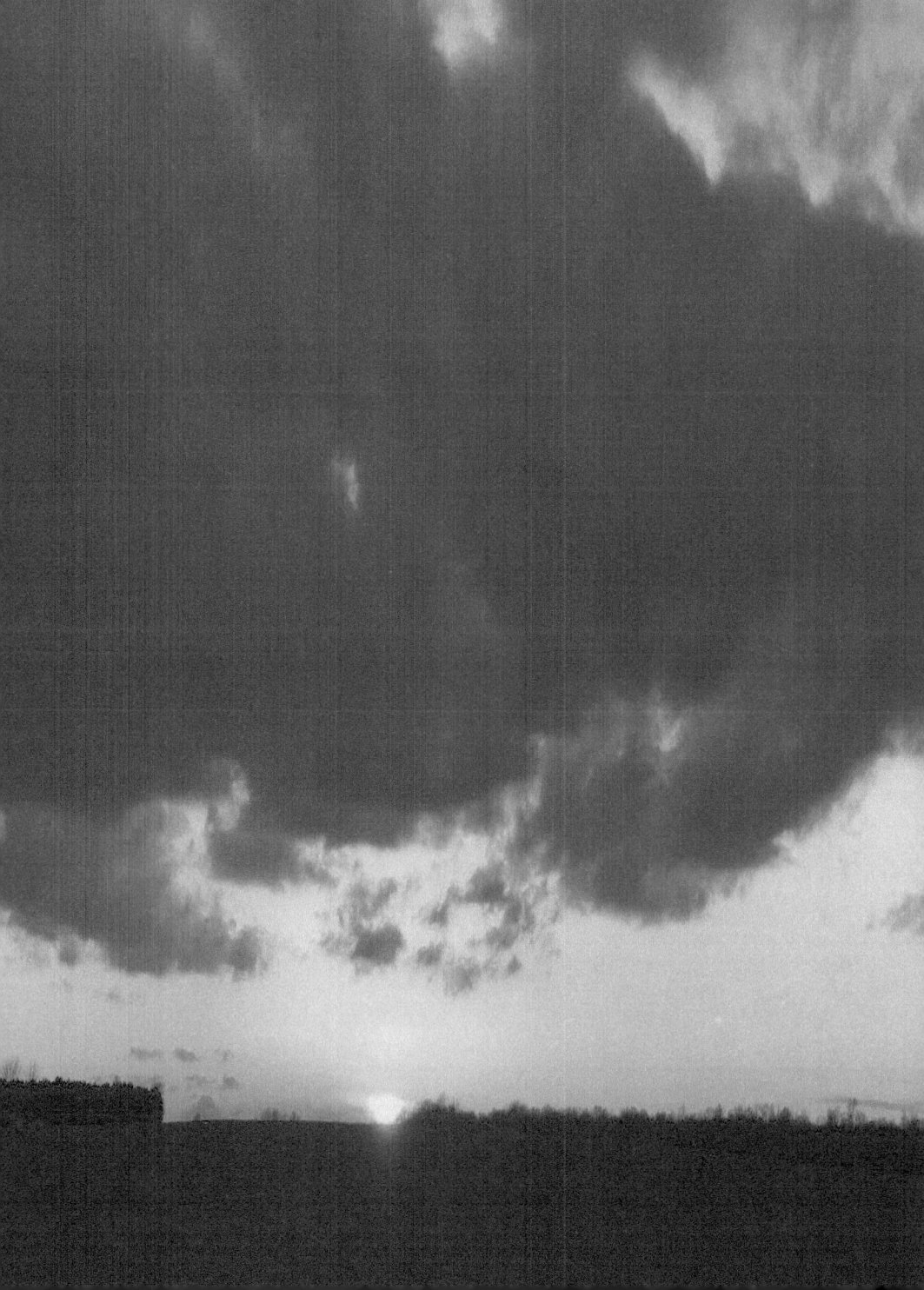

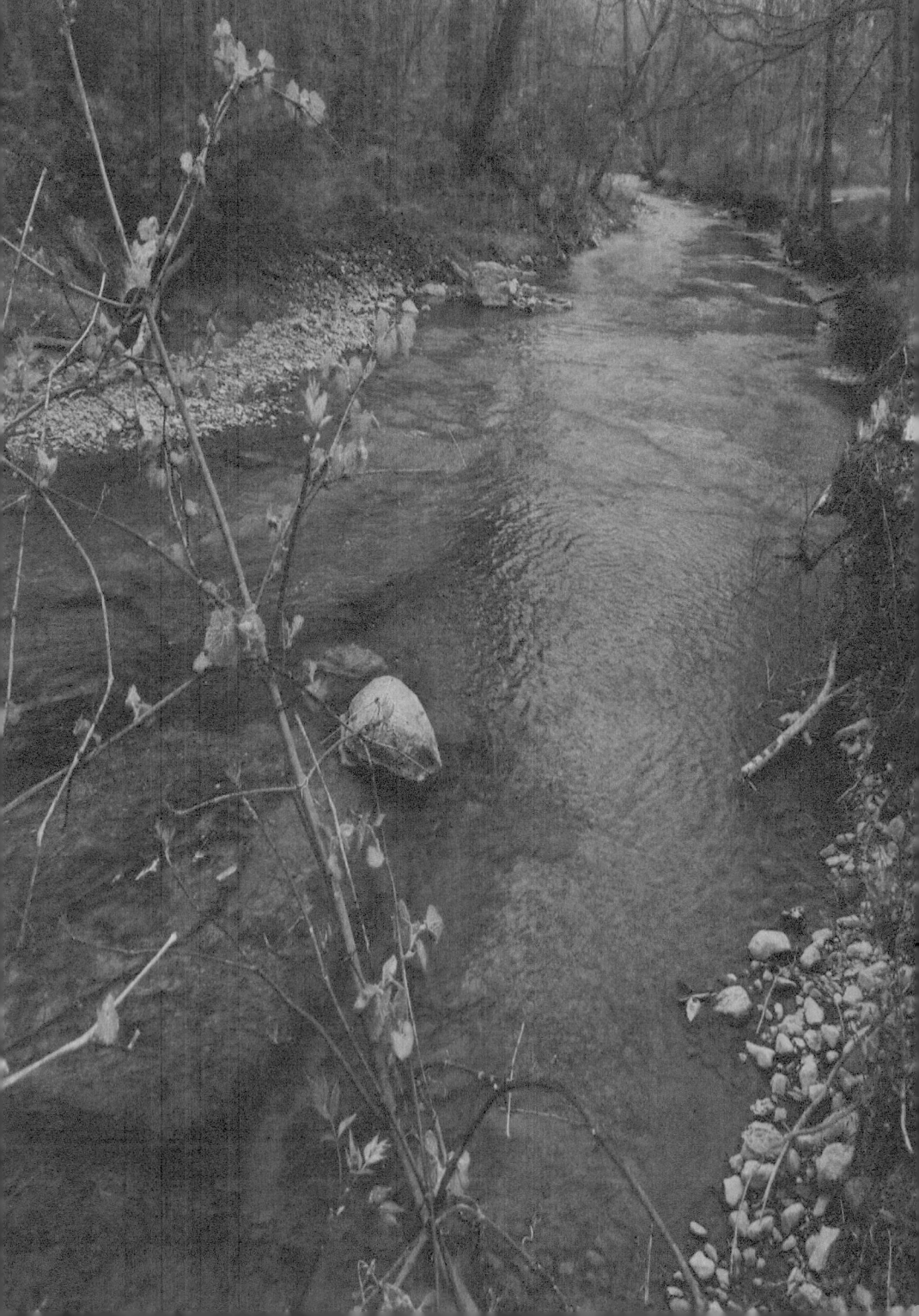

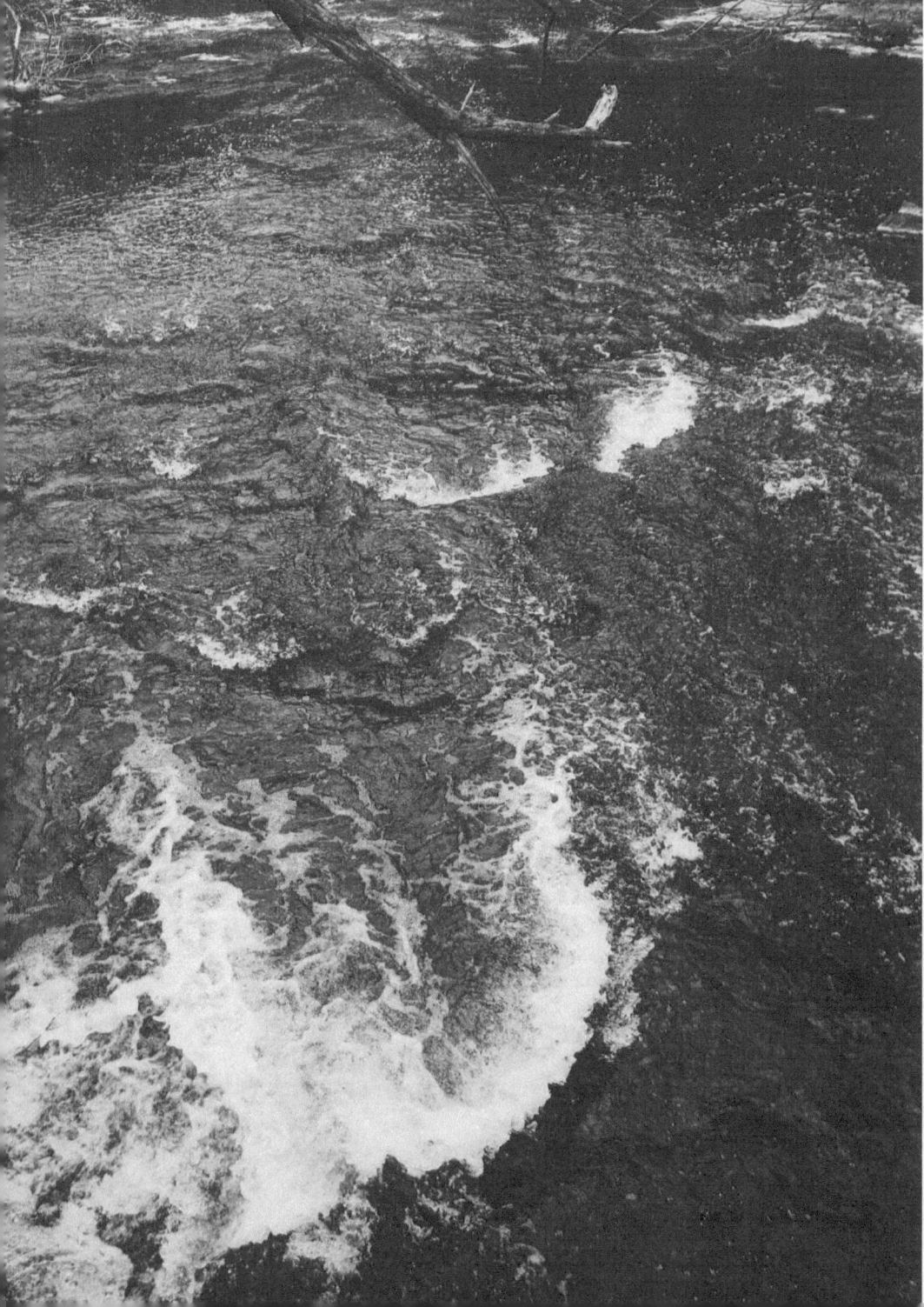

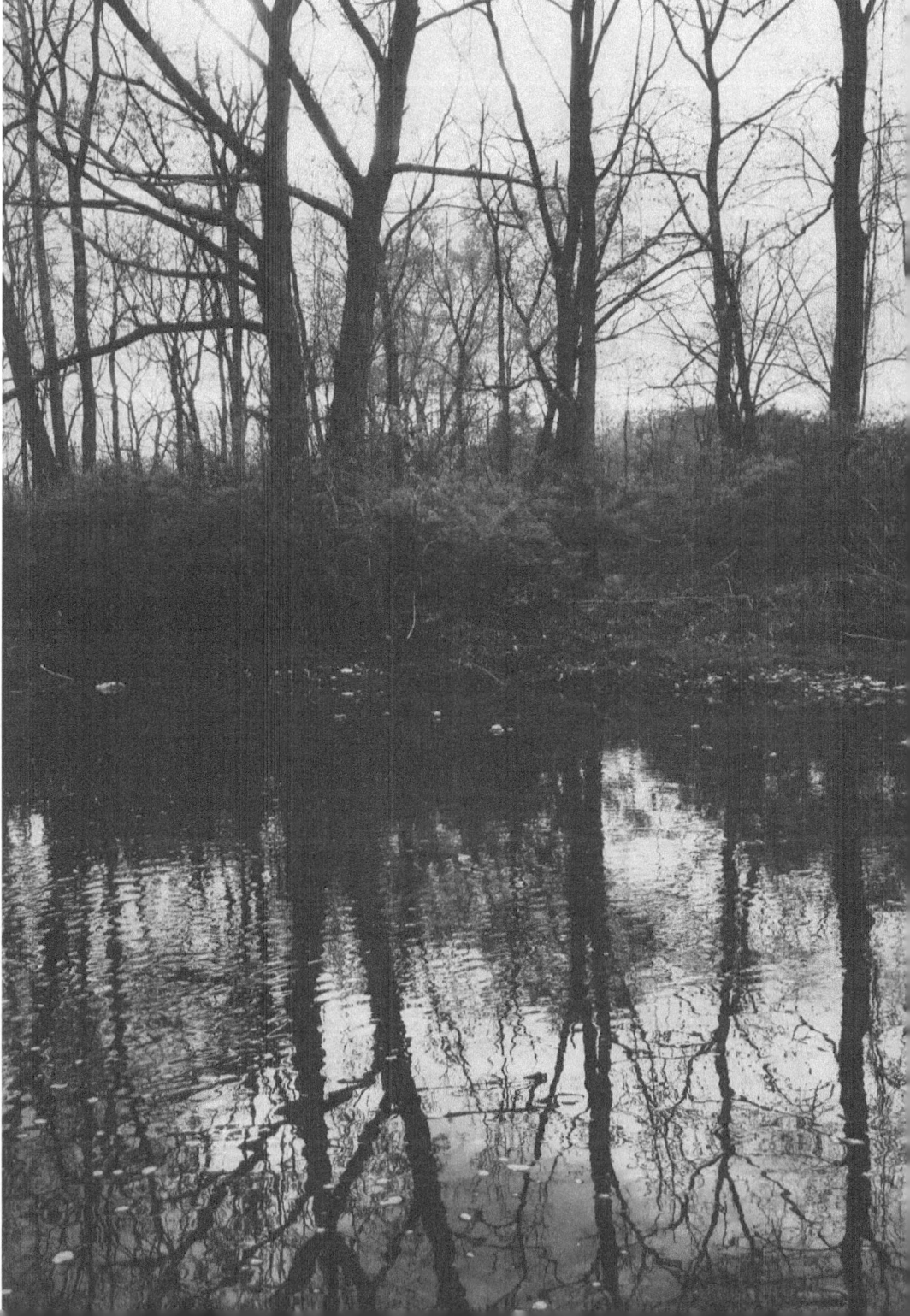

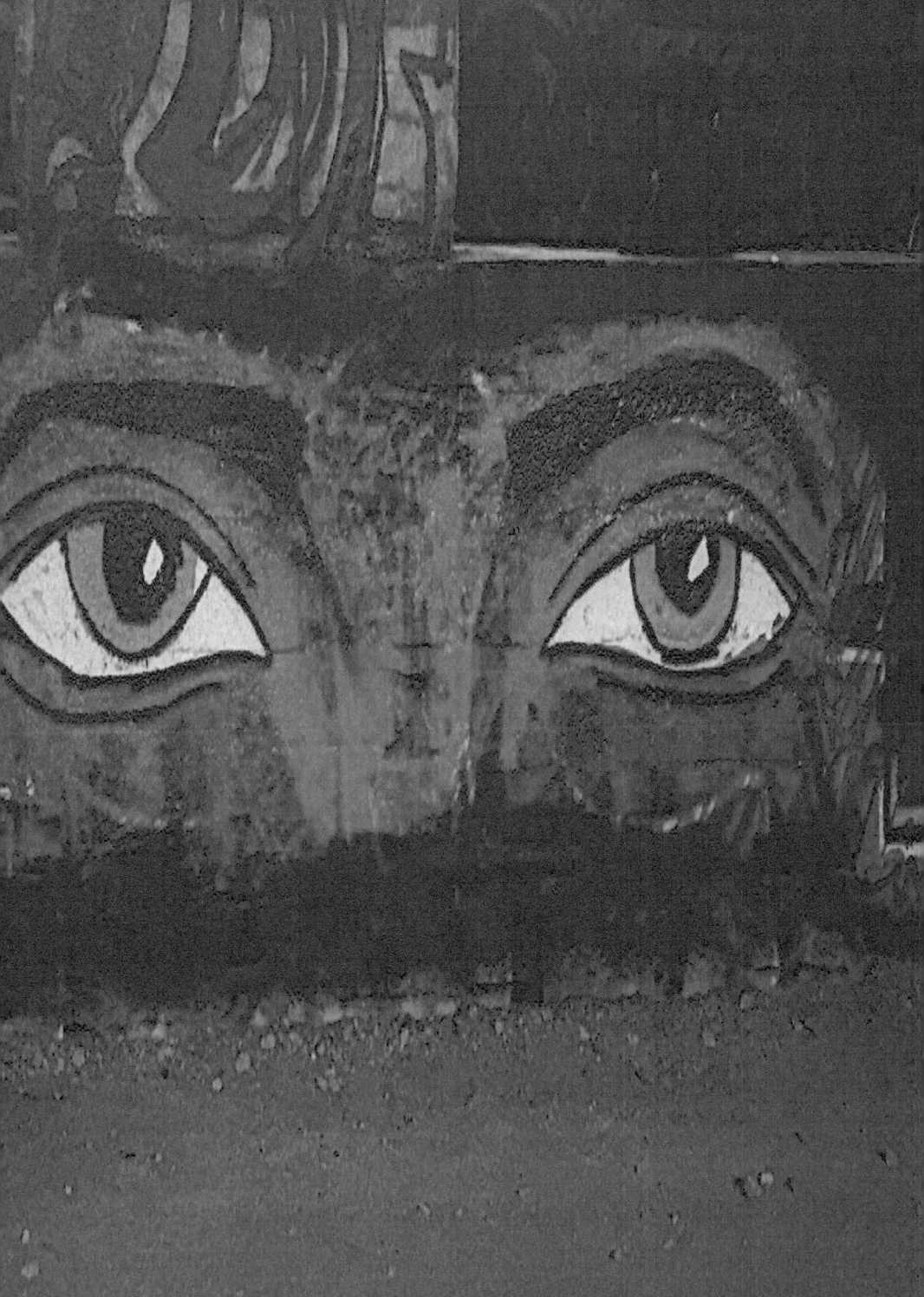

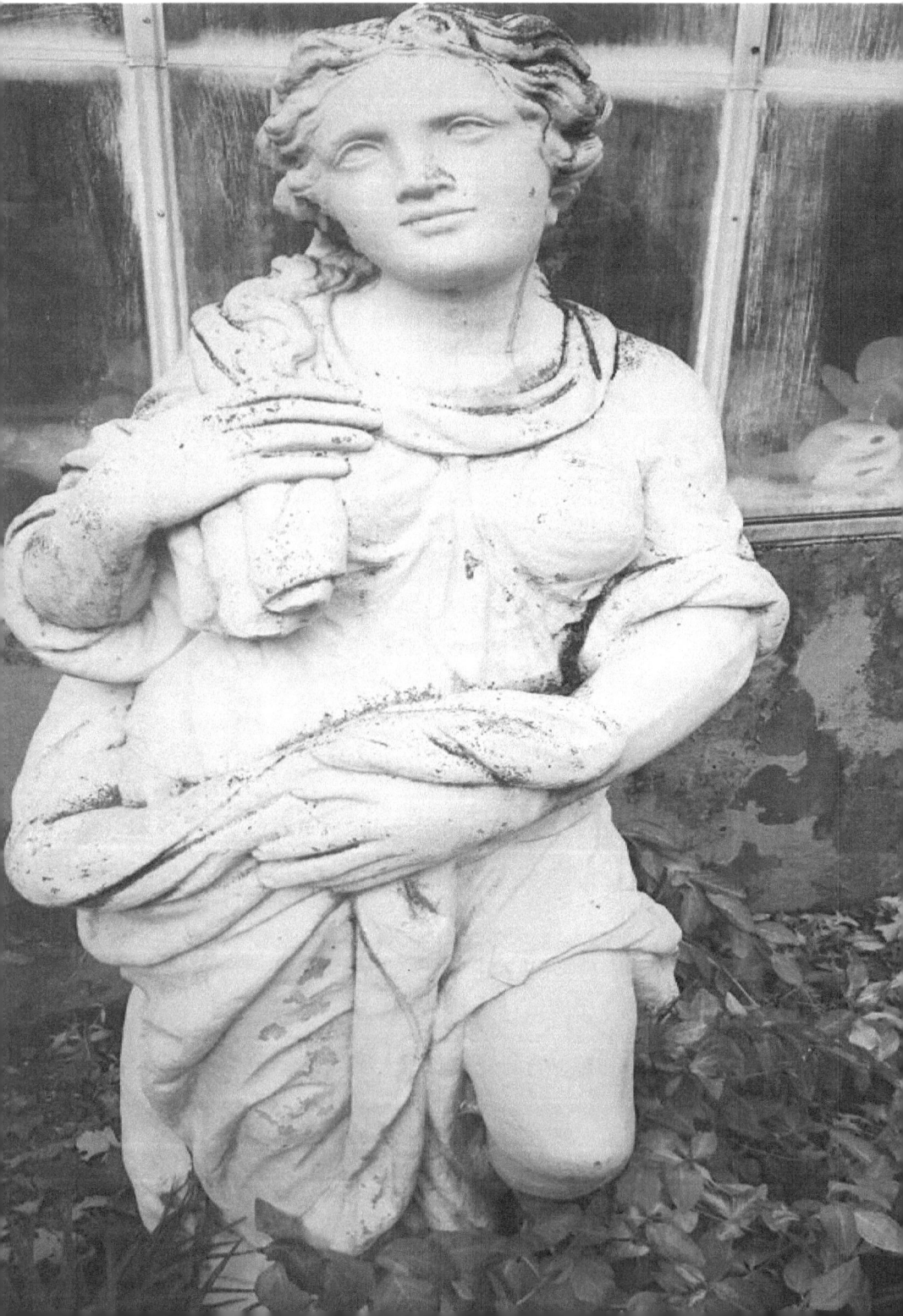

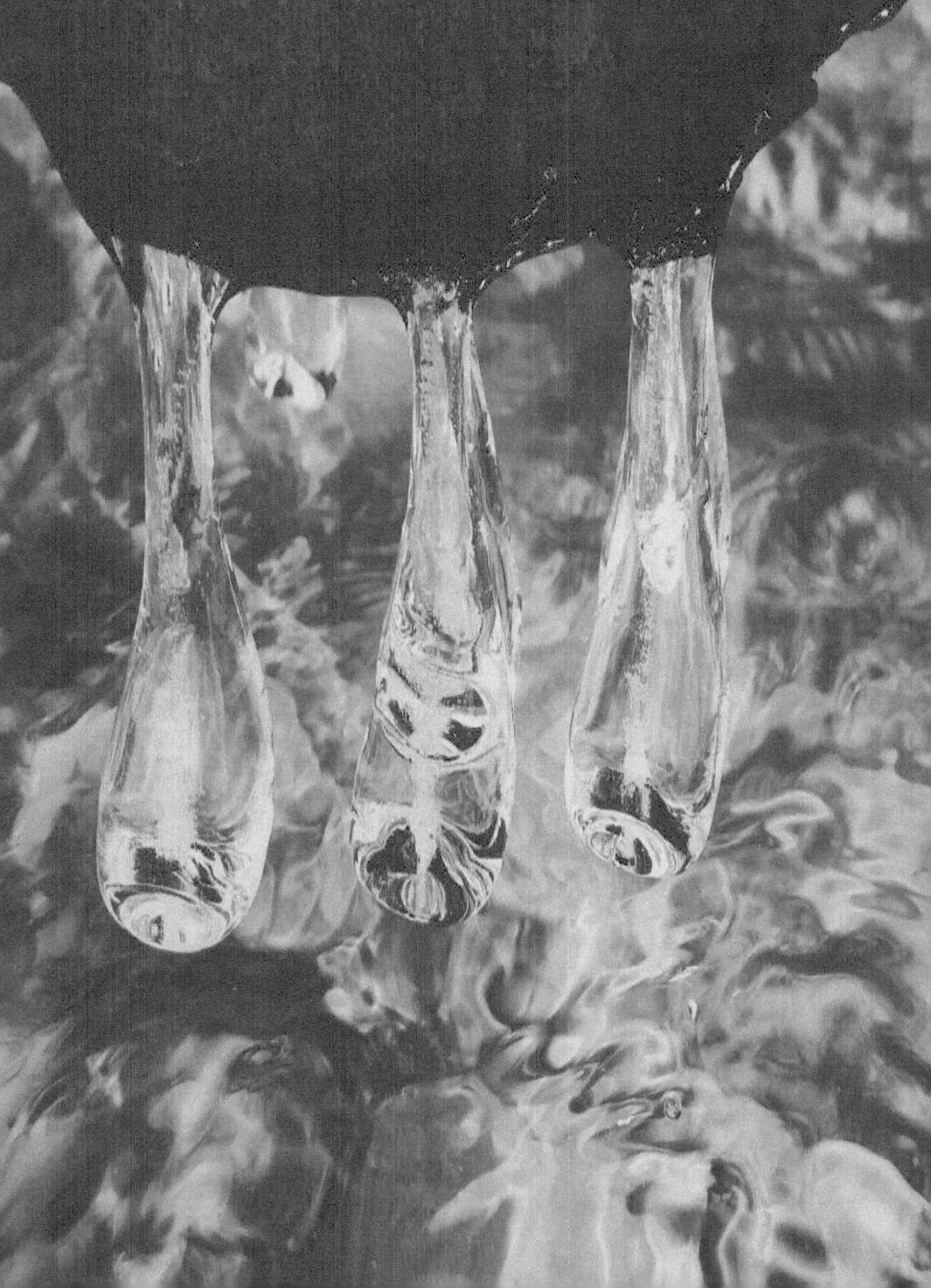

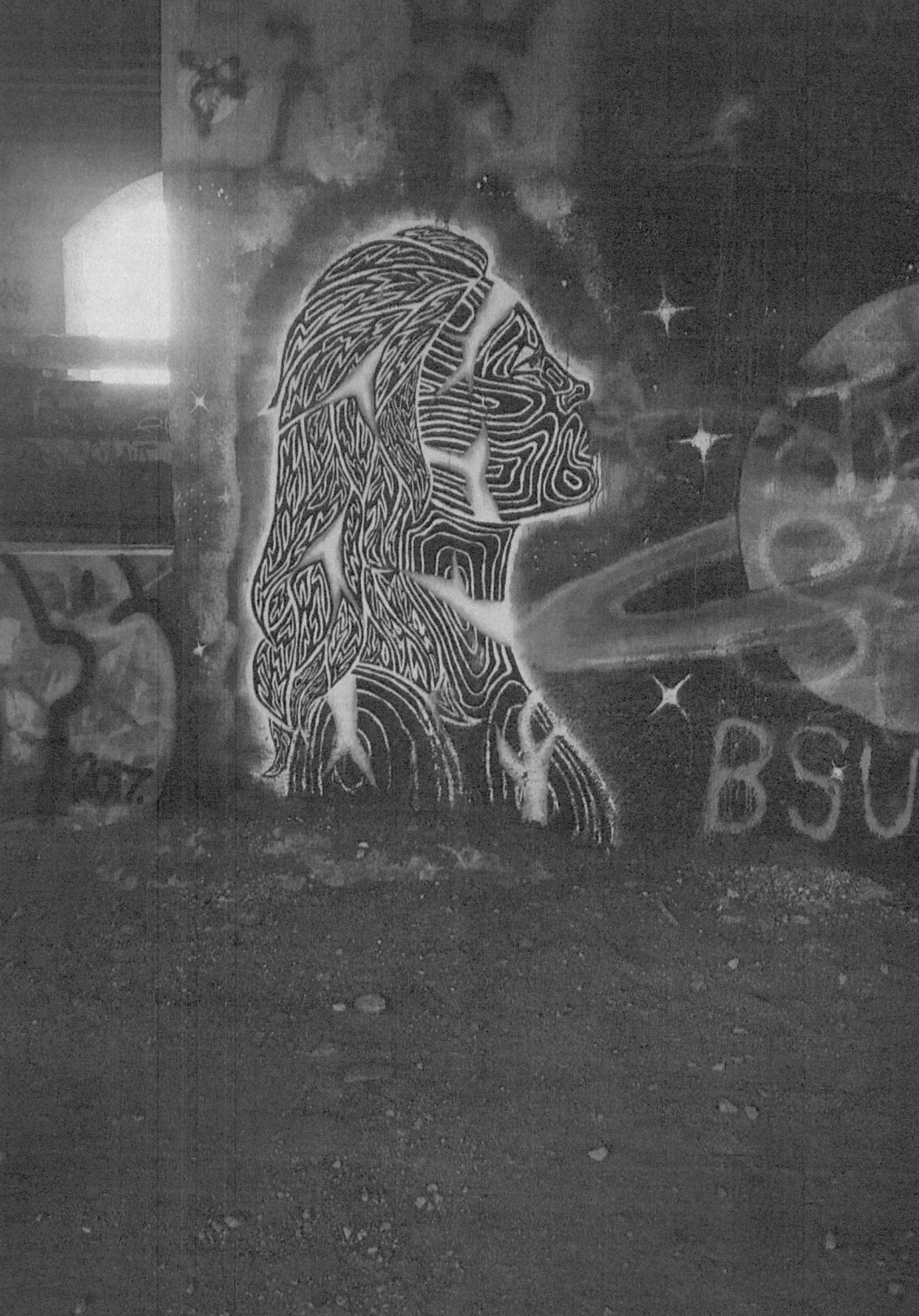

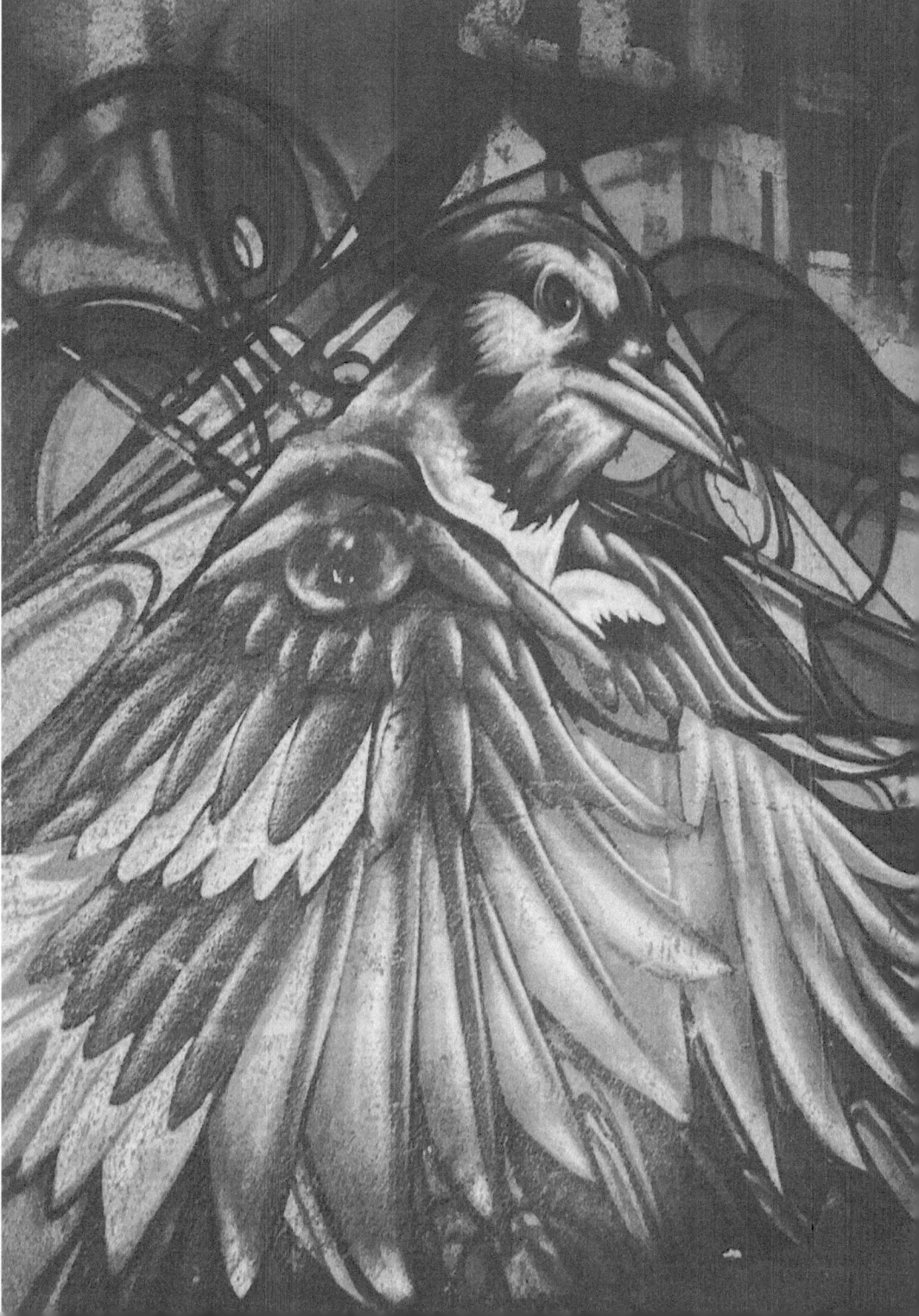

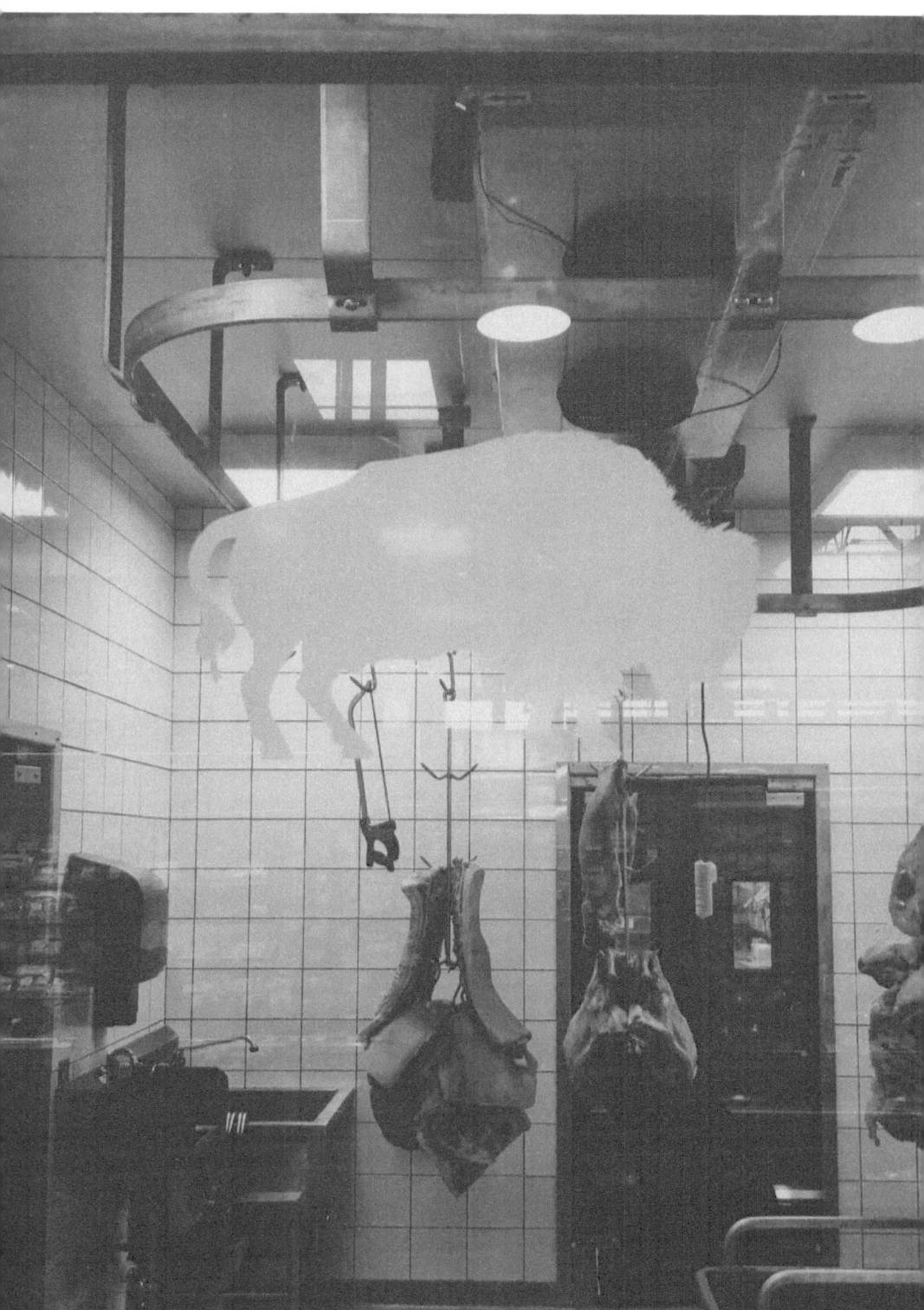

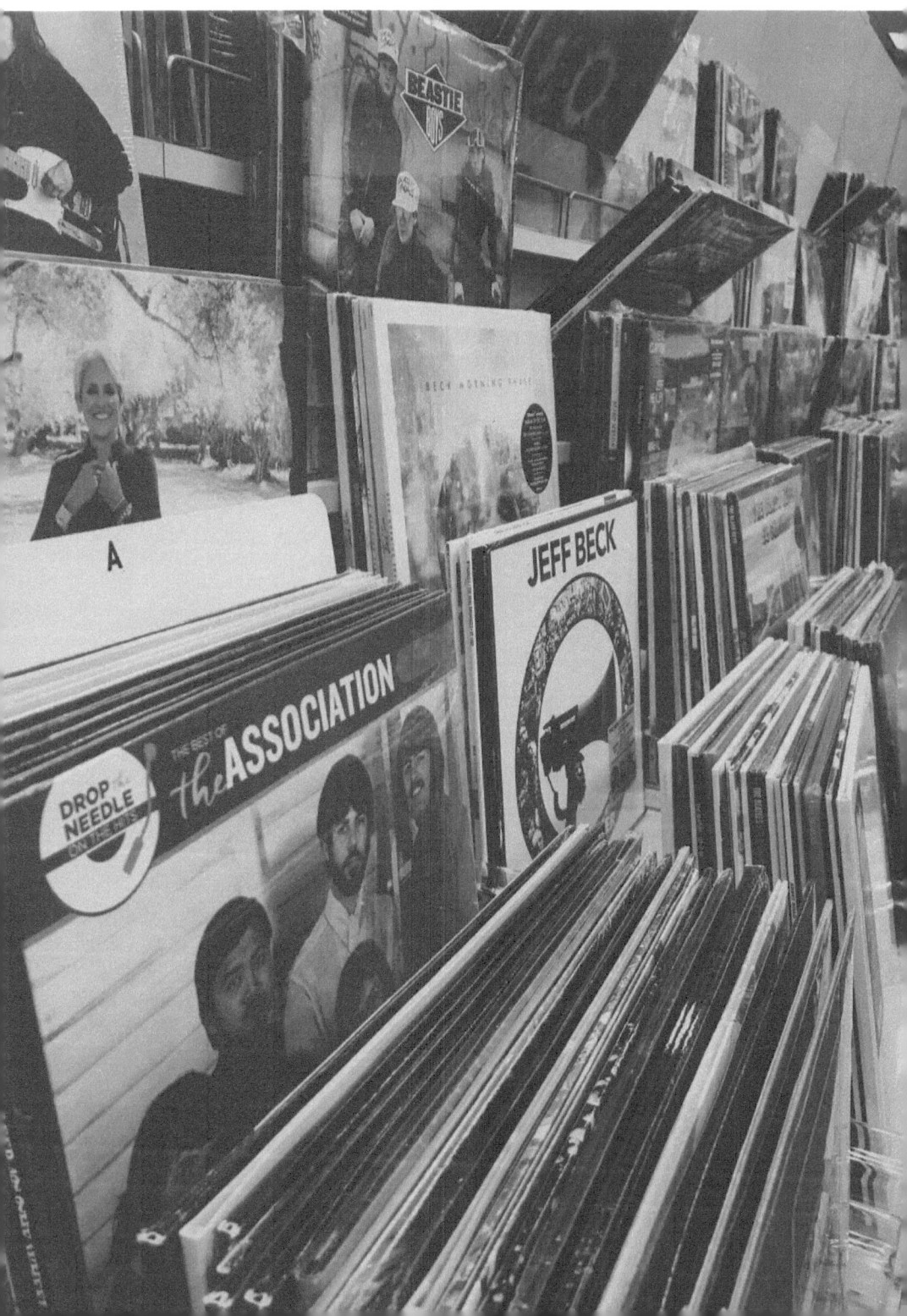

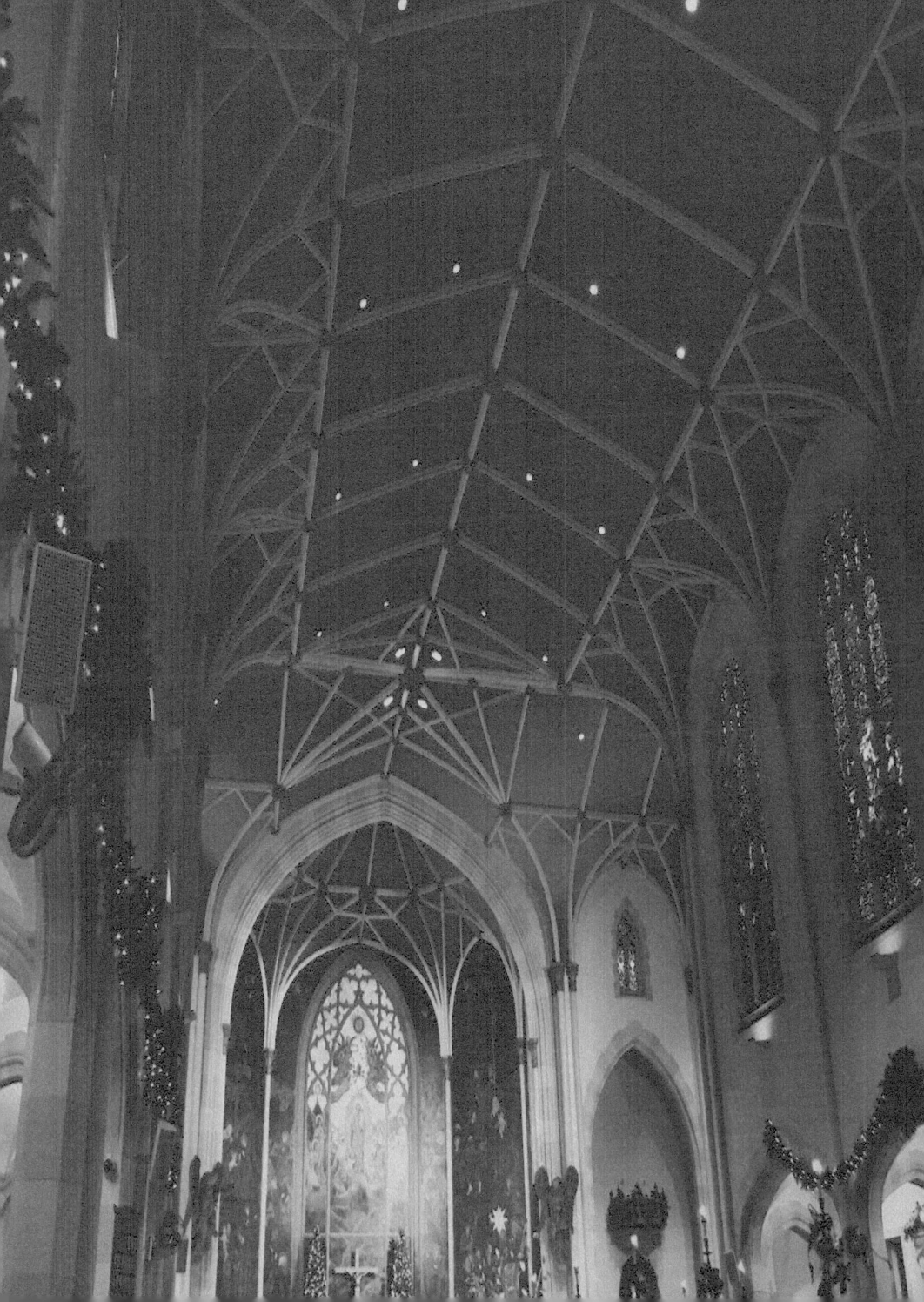

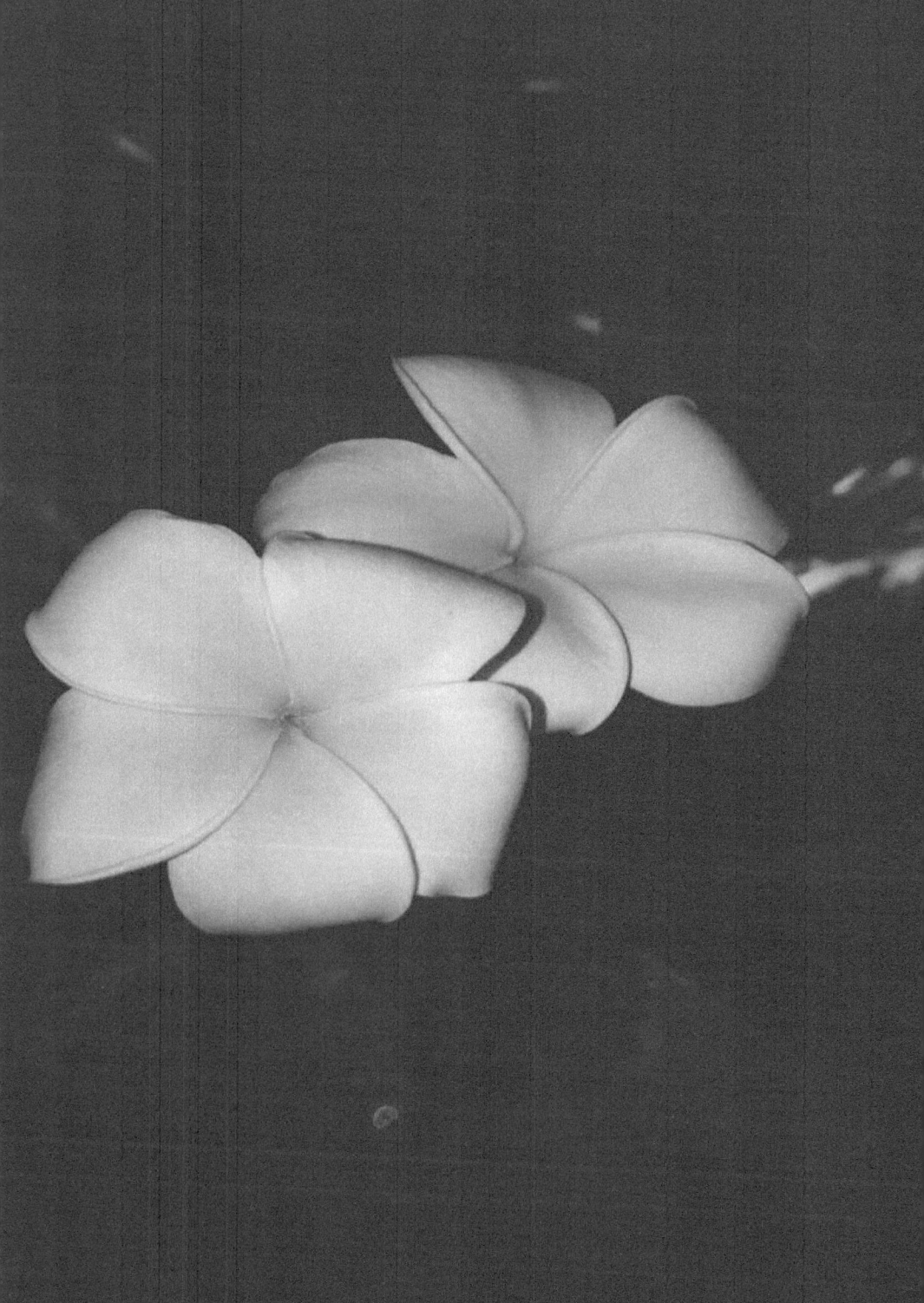

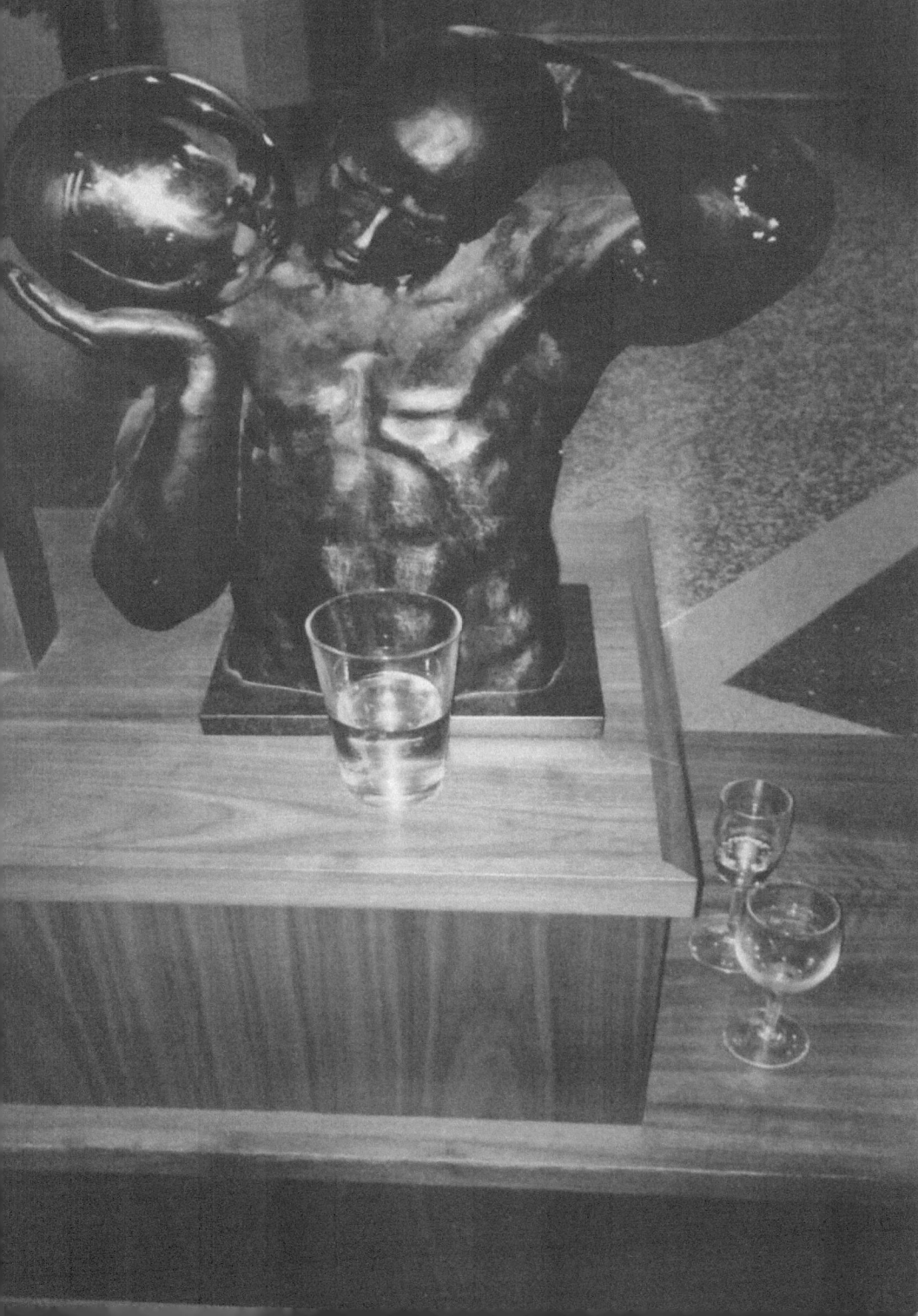

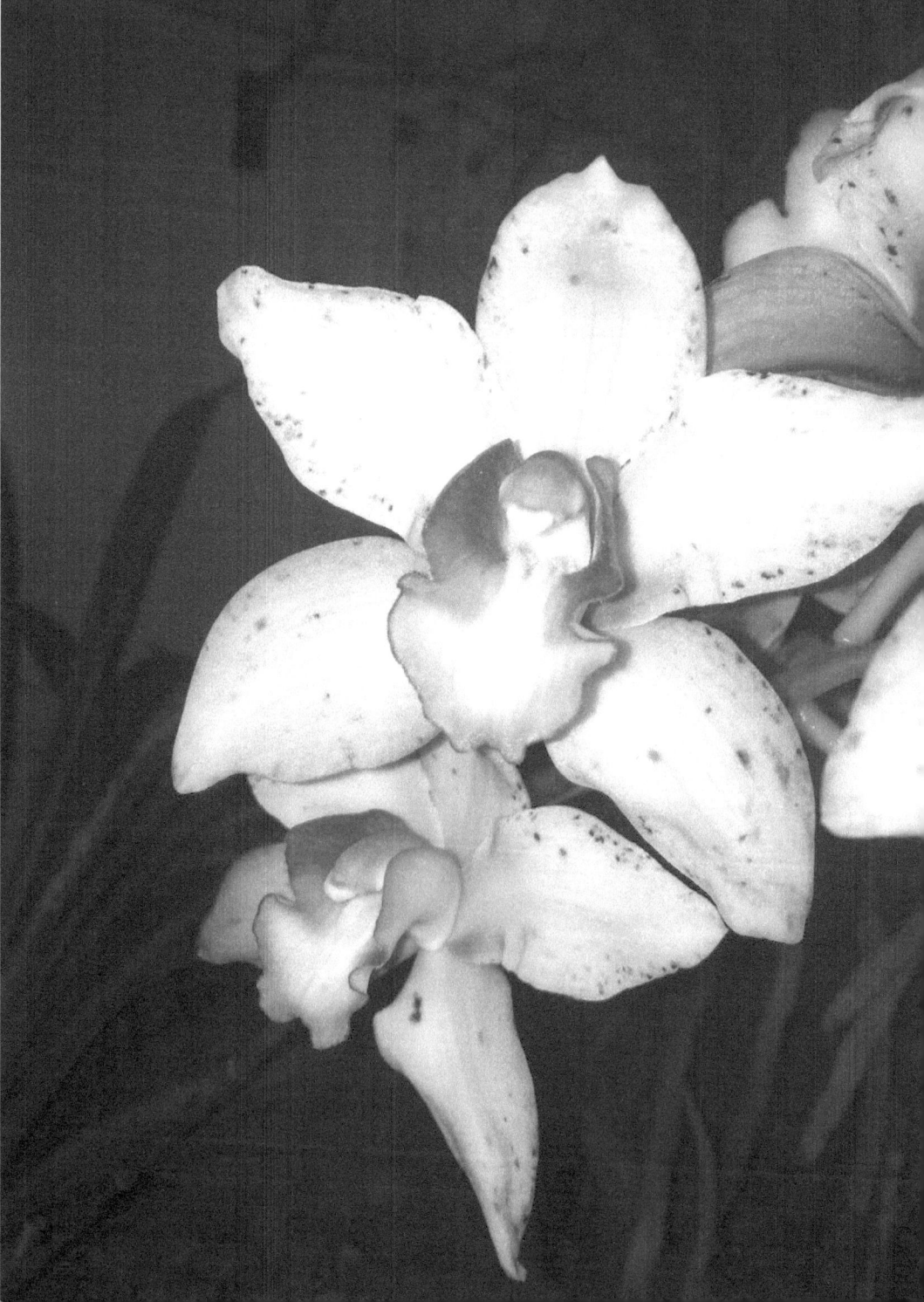

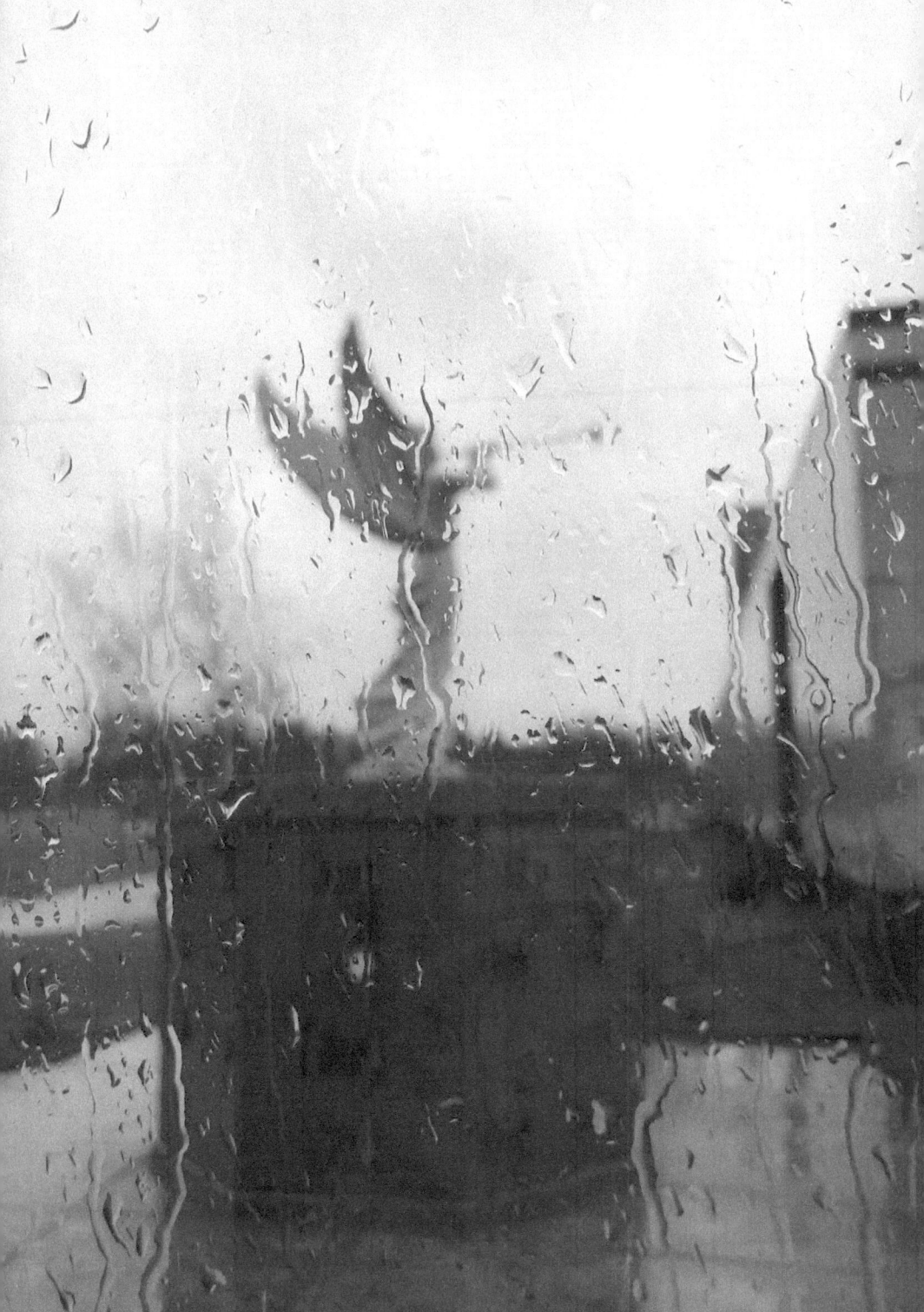

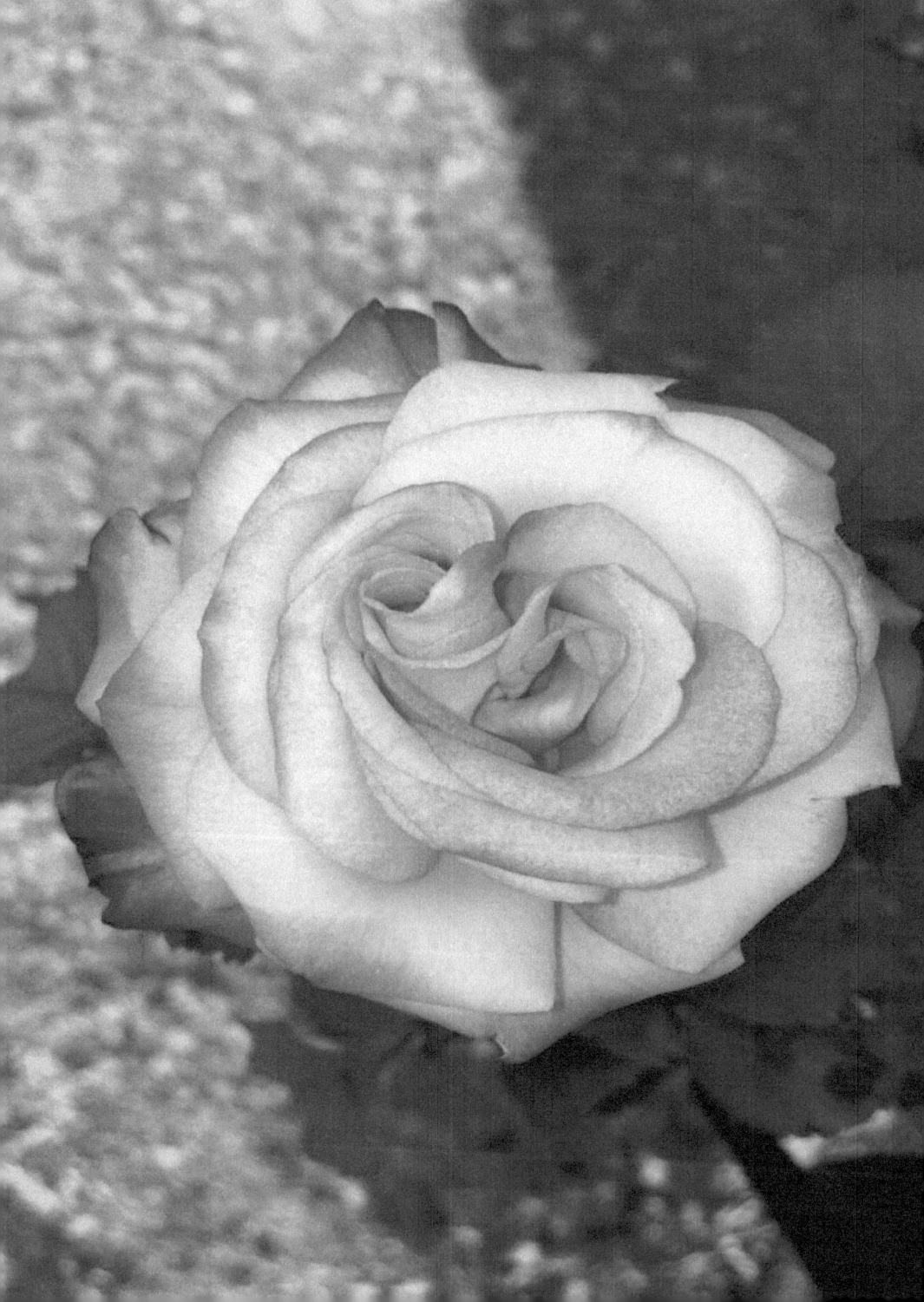

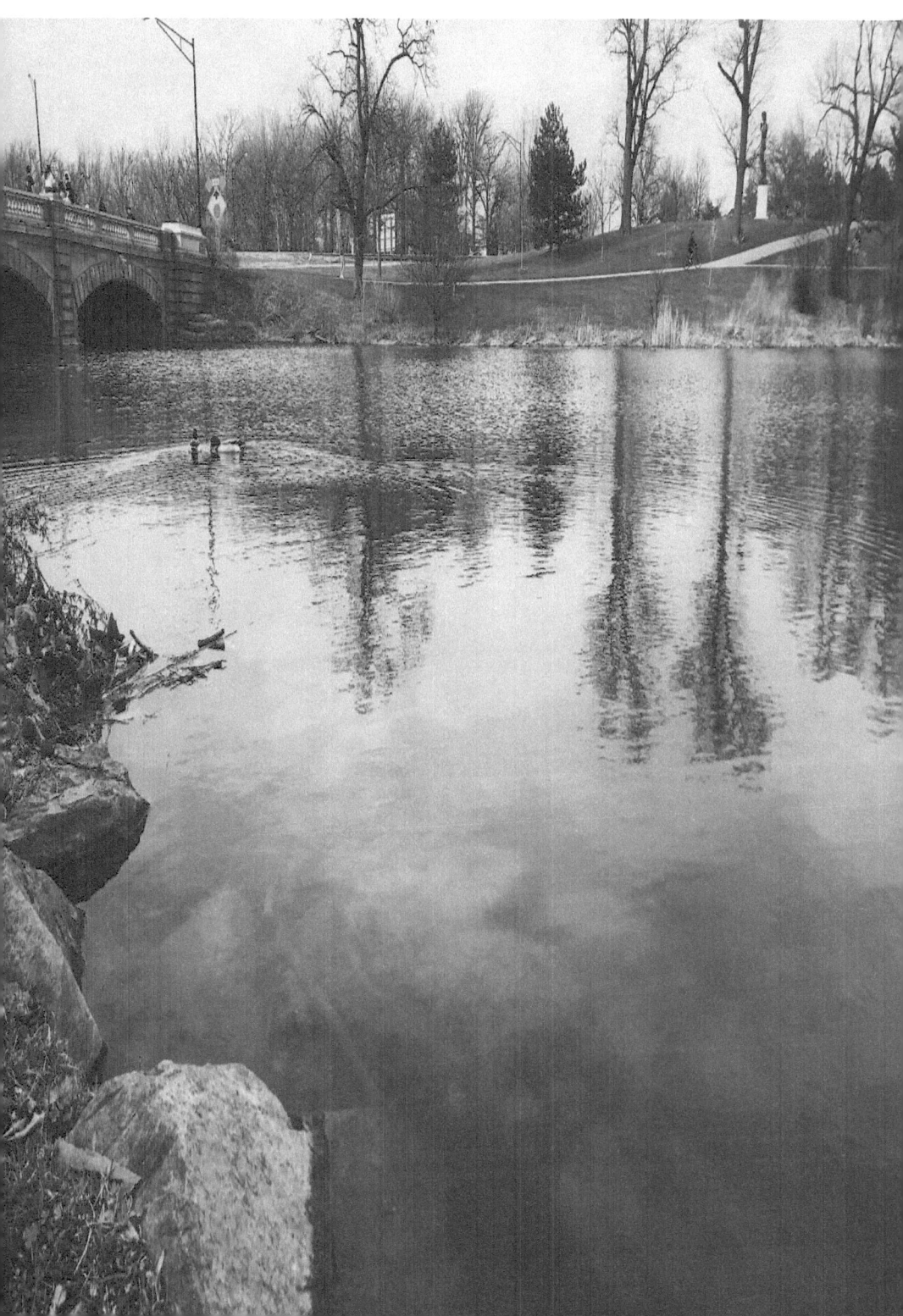

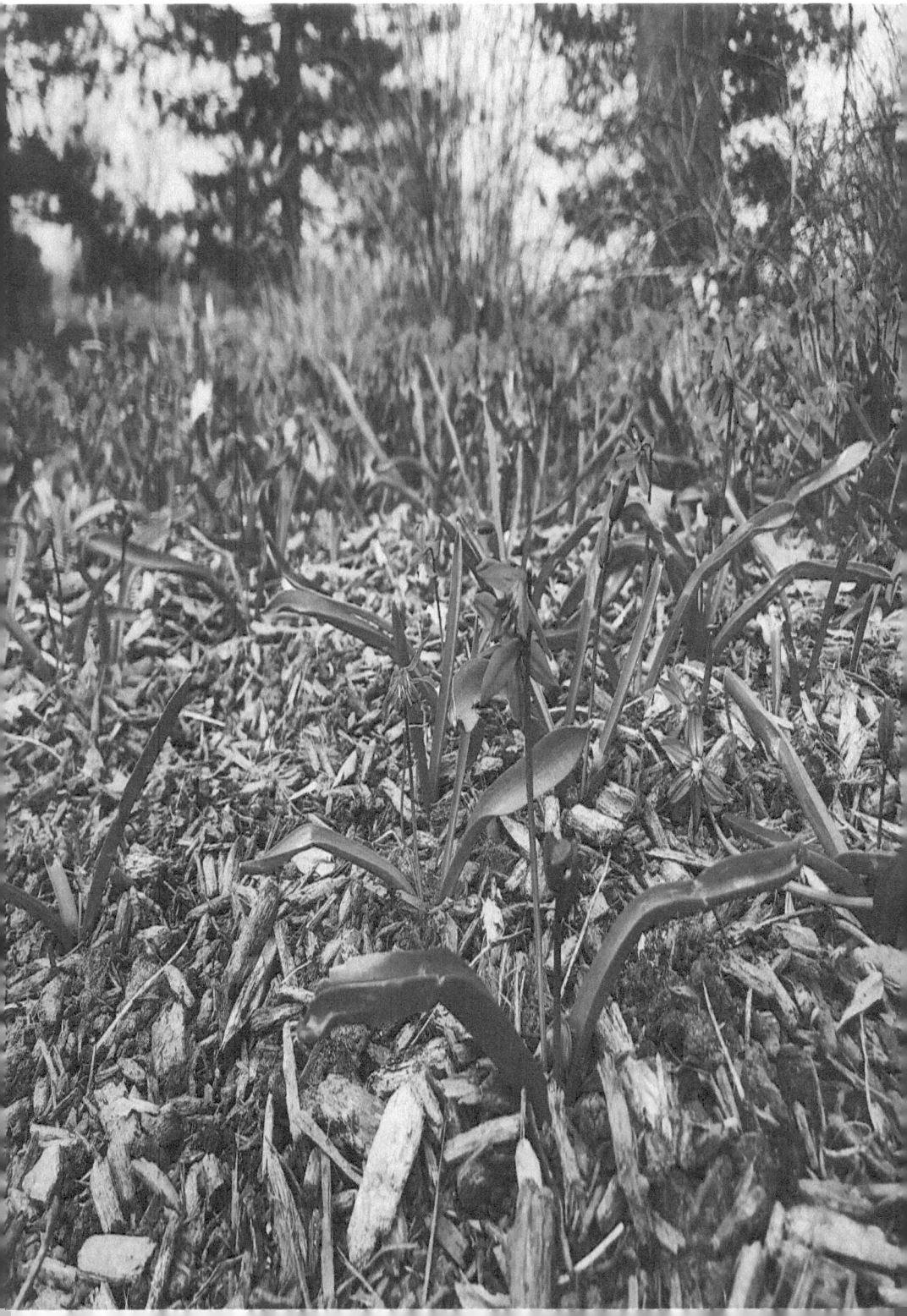

Acknowledgements

i'd like to take this opportunity to say
thank you:
 to my family, for pushing me to go to
school and never give up on the things that
make me happy
to my friends, for always supporting my
creative endeavors and being my muses
to anyone who has ever given me criticism
(positive or negative), for teaching me
growth and how to think outside the box
most importantly, thank you to my mother
for supporting my short stories on the
swingset in our backyard and for buying
my first camera; it's because of you that i
had the courage to write this in the first
place. i love you.

~i.n.l

www.ingramcontent.com/pod-product-compliance
Lightning Source LLC
Chambersburg PA
CBHW021048180526
45163CB00005B/2328